Chrysanthemum Girl

Rosalind,
   I appreciate your haircuts, and more importantly your friendship.
        Frances

FRANCES SNYDER

NEWMAN SPRINGS PUBLISHING
320 Broad Street
Red Bank, NJ 07701

First originally published by Newman Springs Publishing 2019

ISBN 978-1-64096-782-3 (Paperback)
ISBN 978-1-64096-783-0 (Digital)

Printed in the United States of America

Main Characters

Name	Meaning	Character
Atsuko Oshiro	kind child, warm child	narrator, seventeen years old
Harumi Oshiro	spring beauty	younger sister, thirteen years old
Arisu Oshiro	noble (Japanese for *Alice*)	Mama, middle-aged
Hiroshi	generous, tolerant, prosperous	Uncle, Mama's older brother
Maiko	dancing child	Aunt, married to Hiroshi
Mamoru	protector	overseer, elderly
Yuriko	rare child	married to Mamoru, maid
Sayuri	lily	Atsuko's best friend, seventeen
Gorou	fifth son	young man of village, twenty-one
Tadashi	loyal, true	pilot in Imperial Army

Prologue

I grew up surrounded by the ghosts of my ancestors. According to Mama these spirits were present on our small island and we needed to pay attention and give them respect. Most of the time I doubted their existence, but one night I was sure they came after me. I was twelve years old, and it was a night six years before we lost everything...

Darkness hovered on the edges of an October evening as we walked along the road home, a farm two miles out of town. I felt a tug on my jacket and a small hand grabbed my larger one.

"Atsuko, I'm scared." My little sister Harumi's voice quavered.

That didn't surprise me. It was late when we left Aunty Maiko's, and the familiar road appeared threatening in the increasing gloom.

"Don't be afraid—this is the same road we always walk." I spoke with the assurance of an older sister toward someone four years younger. "Let's talk about how much fun we had today. What did you like best about our visit with Aunty Maiko?"

"The food—no, the dolls—and I liked her stories." Harumi started to list all the things we saw and did. "Oh, and don't you think she looked beautiful?"

True. Aunty Maiko greeted us at her door wearing a traditional and very elegant kimono. Embroidery of birds, fishes, and flowers covered the green silk gown. Compared to her, Harumi and I looked plain in the dark skirts and blazers of our school uniforms.

Unlike my parents, who were farmers, Aunty Maiko and Uncle Hiroshi worked in the center of town. They owned a grocery store and lived above it. Harumi and I had been invited to afternoon tea, just the two of us—as though we were grown-up. This was very exciting for us. Our aunt and uncle had recently moved to Okinawa all the way from Kyoto, and we were just getting acquainted with them. This was going to be an opportunity for us to learn more about our aunt. When school let out, we hurried the short distance to the Seijitsu Market and climbed the wooden staircase at the back of the building leading to their apartment.

We had a splendid tea. On a short table, Aunty Maiko set out a teapot shaped like a golden dragon with matching cups. A tray filled with different *wagashi* sat next to the teapot, and we helped ourselves to the colorful desserts. We ate *mochi* stuffed with sweet bean paste and *mitsumame* covered with peaches.

After tea, Aunty Maiko showed us her treasures. She and Uncle Hiroshi had traveled to faraway places—Hong Kong, Paris, and London, among others. Behind the glass of a cabinet, dolls Uncle Hiroshi bought for her stood on display. Aunty Maiko unlocked the doors and took out the dolls and let us hold them. With painted faces and dressed in costumes from faraway countries, each doll had its own story. Aunty Maiko told us about them—either about the dolls themselves or their purchase.

I liked the doll from Scotland best. She had red hair and wore a thick, pleated skirt Aunty Maiko called a kilt. A long scarf in the same pattern of red, brown, and tan squares as the kilt was draped over her shoulder. Aunty Maiko said that she and Uncle Hiroshi had gone to an event called a highland festival, where young girls danced, wearing these costumes.

Harumi's favorite doll came from Paris. She had a name—Marie Antoinette—and wore an elaborate gown, and her hair was piled high on her head. She was very pale. According to Aunty Maiko, she was a queen who had her head chopped off because the French had a revolution. When Aunty Maiko told us that, Harumi grabbed her neck as if she felt the pain of a blade cutting it.

I loved hearing the stories of my aunt's travels to faraway places. Most of my journeys were limited to the short ferry ride from Iejima to Okinawa. Harumi and I had so much fun with Aunty Maiko the time flew by, and we started home much later than we should have.

The autumn afternoon had become evening when we left, and it grew darker and darker as we trudged home. In contrast, our walk to school in the morning had been pleasant. A short distance past our neighbor Mr. Nishiyama's farm, an old star fruit tree had branches bent with the weight of its ripening bounty. We stopped and picked two of the yellow fruit and bit into them. Under the waxy covering, the sun-warmed star fruit was sweet and juicy. Trees lined the edge of the road leading into town. The morning sun shone through red and gold leaves, dappling us with broken bits of light. Harumi and I shuffled through fallen leaves. But in the evening's gloom, the trees loomed like ominous monsters. Their leaves turned into black hands that waved dire warnings over our heads. I started thinking of Mama's stories about the evil spirits that rose up at night and how just that morning she told us we should get home before nightfall. Even though I told myself I didn't believe in Mama's ghosts, as I strode along, Harumi's hand clutched in mine, I wished we had left town earlier. And we hadn't even reached the lake yet.

After we emerged from the woods, the road passed through a clearing with Lake Nekoyangai on the right. Its namesake—cattails—grew along the south shore. During the daytime, their brown fuzzy tips swayed in the breeze, but we couldn't see them at all in the night. The blue of the water had darkened to the color of ink. Clouds floated across the sky, hiding, and then revealing, the moon. When it was visible, the light from the moon reflected off the jet-black water in eerie, silver fragments. Silence surrounded us. The birds we heard sing in the morning had become mute, and the usual chorus of frogs had disappeared.

"It's so quiet. I don't like it." Harumi edged closer to me and held my hand even tighter than before.

"The birds have gone to bed, Harumi, and the frogs have left for the winter."

"What's that?" Harumi practically jumped on top of me at the sound of a sad groan.

"It's nothing, just two trees rubbing together." I tried to sound brave. I was almost positive it was just the moan of trees as they scraped against each other. Nevertheless, I started to walk a little faster.

Then the clouds separated completely. The moonlight made the surface of the lake visible. Trails of mist rose from the water; the hazy wisps grew and started to float toward us. In the shadows, the cattails became the fingers of evil spirits beckoning us.

That's when my bravery deserted me. I froze at the imagined touch of an icy thumb running down my spine while bony fingers squeezed my heart. Those arms of mist reaching out for us would wrap themselves around our legs and suck us into the black, black depths of the lake. They were the sinister ghosts of our ancestors Mama had warned about, and we were destined to be their victims.

Adrenaline surging, I shook off my paralysis. "Let's run!" I yanked Harumi's arm, and we raced down the road. While we were at Aunty Maiko's having tea, I felt plainly dressed in my school uniform, but now I was glad the long skirts of a kimono didn't hamper me. In my short skirt and sturdy shoes, I could easily run away from the spirits that chased me. Poor Harumi, I pulled her so hard she practically flew.

Finally, we left the lake far behind and reached the entry road to our farm. We both were panting as we slowed down to catch our breath.

"My side aches," Harumi said, between loud gasps.

"I know, bend over and breathe slow, it'll feel better."

Shortly after catching our breaths, we went into the house. I had been fearful of Mama's anger over our lateness, but I was so grateful to be safe, the extra chores didn't bother me at all.

That was 1938. I remembered the incident when my country's war came to Okinawa and the evil spirits returned. They flew overhead and marched through our villages. Not the imagined monsters of a frightened girl, these demons were real. When they arrived, we hid.

1944

Chapter 1

Even though clouds filled the February sky, no rain fell, and I decided to work in the small field where I planted peanuts every year. With a hoe, a trowel, and the *bento* Mama packed with my lunch, I walked down our driveway and across the dirt road. I glanced toward both directions. To the right, the road wound through a small wood before reaching our village; to the left, it ended at the edge of our property where a path began that led down to Iwa Cove. The road was empty; not many people passed by our farm.

For the first few hours I worked without interruption—breaking up clumps of soil with my hoe and going back to loosen dirt with a trowel. The noise I made tilling the soil was accompanied by birds that announced their presence—the hoarse shrieks of reef egrets wading in the cove, and the panicked cry of a pigeon caught in midflight by a sparrow hawk. Planes flew steadily overhead. Hidden by the clouds, their throbbing engines were a somber reminder of their mission—traveling to unknown destinations, carrying soldiers to their deaths.

By noontime I was stiff and hungry; I stopped working and straightened up to stretch when I heard my name called.

"Atsuko! Atsuko!"

"Sayuri! I'm so glad to see you!" I smiled as my friend left the road and crossed the field to join me. "I wasn't expecting you. This is wonderful." We used to be together every day, but our school had closed four months earlier, and neither one of us enjoyed much leisure. I put down the hoe and wiped my hands on my shirt. "I need a rest, and it's time for lunch. You can join me." We walked over to the

Ryukyu Pine growing along the edge of the field and sat down. I let my muscles relax as I leaned against the trunk.

"You work too hard. We all work too hard," Sayuri said.

"This isn't bad. I'm preparing the soil so I can plant peanuts—just as I've done every year." I picked up the *bento* and opened it. I wasn't expecting much—our food had become increasingly scarce—but was surprised to see Mama had packed *onigiri*. The four rice balls, wrapped with small strips of seaweed, would make a welcome meal, and there was enough to share.

"Looks as though these two are filled with pickled carrots and the other two have *kabocha*. We can eat one of each kind. Oh! Did Mama know you were coming? She packed two napkins." I shrugged when Sayuri shook her head no. It wasn't the first time I thought my mother had an extra sense for what was needed. I handed Sayuri the box so she could remove her two rice balls. We both ate the carrot *onigiri* first and the one filled with squash second. It was sweeter. I chewed slowly, to make the meal seem bigger. "You're not working today?"

"My father gave me the day off." Sayuri winced.

"What's wrong?"

"It's difficult doing the jobs of men."

"True, but you look as though you are in pain."

She looked at me, and it appeared as though she were about to cry. "What do you think is going to happen to us? I feel as if all of Japan is going to be destroyed. I'm scared—all of the time."

"Me too. Earlier today I saw a sparrow hawk grab a pigeon in its talons and carry the bird away. The pigeon didn't do anything to deserve such a cruel end. That's how we are—defenseless—just like that poor bird."

"I want to show you something." Sayuri lifted her shirt, revealing her stomach. An angry-looking bruise, about two inches wide, made a dark purple stripe across her body.

"Oh! What happened? Did someone beat you? Here, rest against the tree." I moved so she could have more of the trunk to lean on. "Are you in pain? Of course you are." My horror over Sayuri's injury had me babbling. "Tell me what happened."

"Yesterday—on the ferry. I was holding a chain when the boat bumped into the pilings. The collision caused me to let go of the chain, and somehow it whipped across my body. I fell down."

"That's why your father gave you the day off—to heal. Is he giving you any more time?"

"No. My absence today makes a hardship for Papa. He doesn't have anybody else to help. He's afraid if he can't keep the ferry running, he'll lose his job."

"You shouldn't have come today. You should have stayed home and rested."

"It's impossible for me to do nothing for a whole day, and Mama kept fussing over me. It doesn't hurt that much to walk." Sayuri looked at me with a stubborn expression I knew well. "Please forget about my silly complaints. My stomach looks worse than it is. My ribs and my insides feel all right—I'm sure I'll heal quickly. And this is better than being in the army." Then her look of determination faded, and two tears rolled down her cheeks.

"You are hurt! I can take you to Mama—"

"No. It's not the pain. It's Junichi and Nobu—we don't know what's happening."

"The mail is terrible. Do you even know where your brothers are?"

"No. We only heard once, last summer. Nobu wrote they were fine, but not allowed to tell us anything about where they were or what they were doing."

"How are your parents dealing with it?"

"The strain is terrible. Papa doesn't say much. His jaw is so tight, it's as though he has a lock on it. Mama isn't eating, and she's gotten so thin. I hear her crying at night. Every time we learn about a battle, we wonder if Junichi and Nobu are fighting, or if they are even alive. We're living with a big black weight pressing on us, and no way to get rid of it."

"Oh, I'm so sorry. Is there anything I can do?"

"Just be my friend." Sayuri took a deep breath and wiped her face. "It's a relief to have someone to talk to. But let's talk about you now. Is there anyone to help with the peanuts?"

"Harumi comes home this evening. She has a two-week break from school."

"How does she like staying on Okinawa? And her new school?"

"I'm sure she'll tell me tonight." I gave a short laugh. "When Maryknoll Academy closed here, Harumi was sure it meant no more school for her, and she started to celebrate. Then Mama ruined Harumi's happiness when she told her about the arrangement with the Kinjo family in Ginoza."

"Too bad you couldn't go as well."

"Mama needs me here. I keep telling myself when the war is over, I can go back to school—maybe even go to university." I stood up and grabbed the hoe and trowel. "I need to get back to work. Can you stay a little longer? And keep me company while I work?" When she agreed and sat on a mound of dirt to watch, I knew she must be hurting more than she let on.

"It doesn't look too difficult—the soil is sandy." Sayuri picked up a handful and sifted the dirt through her fingers.

"Good dirt for growing peanuts."

"Why do you use the trowel?"

"I don't have to dig too deep." I held my thumb and forefinger about an inch apart. "The seeds are planted shallow."

"Do you have enough seeds? What are they like?"

"Yes, I have a whole bagful." I laughed. "You are not a farmer—peanut seeds are peanuts. Raw peanuts I saved from last year."

"Will you sell your crop again this year?"

"I don't think so. It's better to have the food than the money I could make."

"I know what you mean. I went to the Seijitsu Market last week, and the shelves were mostly empty."

"Uncle Hiroshi and Aunty Maiko are closing their market. Uncle Hiroshi says it's impossible to stock the store. The rice we ate for lunch was from one of the last bags he had."

"It was good rice. Better than the bag my mother bought on Okinawa. It was mostly dirt, and when I cleaned the rice, I found dead bugs and mouse droppings." Sayuri grimaced.

"So, what are your aunt and uncle going to do?"

"Come live with us. Uncle Hiroshi has never farmed, but he says he's happy to help."

"What about your aunt?"

"I don't know. She's very kind, but all the time she's been married, Uncle Hiroshi has treated her like *hime*. He never expected his beautiful wife to work very hard."

"Will that be trouble?"

"I don't think so. Mama likes her sister-in-law, and we're so busy there isn't time for quarrels. We can use the extra help. All we have now are Mamoru and his wife, Yumiko."

"But they're old. How much help are they?"

"What can we do? Everyone else is off fighting."

Sayuri didn't answer my question—after all, what could she say? I stopped digging when two rows remained to be prepared. "Time for me to quit. I'm getting sore." I looked over the small section still needing to be tilled. "I can finish tomorrow morning, and if the weather holds, I'll plant in the afternoon. In four months we should have a good peanut crop. I'll share some of it with you."

"I'd like that. It's getting late, and I should start back home." Sayuri stood and brushed off the dirt clinging to her clothes. "Thanks for listening to me and my silly problems."

"Not silly at all. If you don't start to heal, tell someone—get help. I mean it." I picked up the hoe and trowel while Sayuri tucked the *bento* underneath my arm.

"I'm sure I'll be fine. Don't tell anyone—about what happened to me. Promise?"

"Not even Mama?"

"No one—please?"

"I won't, but it's hard to keep secrets from Mama." We reached the road, and I bobbed my head in a short bow. "Good-bye. Take care of yourself."

"I'll come again, when I can." Sayuri smiled and briefly touched my arm before turning to walk back to town.

After storing the tools, I walked into the house, first removing my outdoor shoes.

"Atsuko, it's good you're back," Mama said. "Harumi will be here soon. Hiroshi is meeting her ferry and will walk with her."

"I'm glad Harumi will be home." I was surprised by how much I meant it. Her absence made me realize how much I appreciated my little sister—with her frank opinions and unpredictable sense of humor. Her antics could always shake me from my more serious moods and make me laugh. I looked forward to the family being together again.

Chapter 2

Mama asked me to feed the chickens before Harumi and Uncle Hiroshi arrived. Hapless birds, they looked as hungry as I felt. I didn't have much grain to throw them, and it was poor quality. Mama had separated the millet and saved the best for us while the chickens received the kernels she couldn't bring to use for our meals. I apologized to the small flock gathered around to pick up the feed I scattered to them. Just like the rest of us, their days of plenty had faded to distant memories. I didn't feel entirely sad; after all, the birds spent all day pecking away at the dirt for insects. However, I did feel a twinge for the creatures, clucking away mindlessly without a thought to their final destination—our dinners. Mama butchered the hens when they quit laying eggs. Butchering a chicken temporarily solved our food shortage; the meat and bones became part of our meals for as long as Mama could make them last.

My sister arrived while I was outside. She must have been eager to be home; I saw her impatience as she walked up the drive with Uncle Hiroshi. She would stride ahead of him, then pause and wait for our uncle, who carried her suitcase and walked slower. When they neared the house I heard Harumi's voice. I couldn't tell what she talked about, but I heard her say *baka* twice. Even though she carried a bag, Harumi swung her arms to emphasize her thoughts. Uncle Hiroshi put his hand on her arm and shook his head. I don't know what he said to her, but her behavior often startled him. He was accustomed to Aunty Maiko with her soft voice and perfect manners. Whatever Harumi talked about, I'm sure Uncle Hiroshi didn't want her to use the word *stupid*. I was glad Harumi didn't stop and sulk when he reprimanded her; instead, she nodded her head, shifted the bag, and continued up the driveway. Since I finished feeding the chickens, I joined them on the front porch where Mama waited.

Inside the entryway to our house, we removed our outdoor shoes.

"Ah, here are my slippers, right where I left them." Harumi smiled as she changed her footwear. "Now my feet feel as though I'm home."

"Pick up your bag. We can take your things to our room." I grabbed the suitcase and led the way down the hall.

"Did you see Uncle Hiroshi scold me? I'm always in trouble. I don't mean to, but everything I do results in disaster." She opened the *tansu* standing in the corner and started to empty the clothes from her bag into the wooden chest that had been in our family since my grandfather's time.

"I don't think you are *always* in trouble." I opened Harumi's suitcase and began handing her its contents. "It probably just seems that way. I know when I was your age, I thought I could never do anything correctly."

"You? Act improperly? You're perfect." Harumi's eyes widened. "I'm always being told I should act more like you. 'Atsuko doesn't run around like a chicken without its head. Atsuko knows when to be quiet. Atsuko has beautiful manners.' I don't think I can ever be like you, no matter how hard I try."

"Why do you want to be like me? We're two different people, and I'm not perfect—not even close."

"That's not the way it feels to me."

"Listen. I'm seventeen, you're still twelve—"

"Almost thirteen."

"Yes, almost thirteen. But that's still a big difference. And look at me. I'm not as beautiful as Aunty Maiko. I can't run the household like Mama—she won't even let me cook anymore. She says we don't have enough food to waste on my failures. I don't talk myself into trouble like you do, but then I can't make people laugh the way you can. I can be too quiet, and you can be too lively. We all have good and bad qualities."

"And my bad qualities really stick out."

"Don't be so hard on yourself, things will improve. Give yourself some time and try to think before you talk. Tell me, what did Uncle Hiroshi say when you were in the driveway?"

"Oh, he doesn't like the word *stupid*. He said a well-mannered girl doesn't use such language. But my new school *is* stupid."

"Why do you think that?"

"The drills—that's all we do, drill, drill, drill."

"But we did drills at the academy." I thought about how we stood at our desks and recited math, history, and literature. "Memorizing is a good way to learn."

"That's not what I mean. We do defense drills."

"Safety practice? What's stupid about that? We are in danger these days."

"Yes, I know. All day long planes fly over. In Ginoza, soldiers march through the streets, we have to obey curfew, and have identification with us always. Now the government teachers think they will save us with our drills."

"Drills can be good."

"Not these. If an enemy plane flies over and drops a bomb, or soldiers shoot at us, we won't be able to protect ourselves. Do you know what we have? Bamboo spears—stupid bamboo spears. We perform outdoor drills with them—three times a day, for an hour each time. I'm now skilled at charging a dummy stuffed with hay and killing it." Harumi pantomimed holding a spear and thrusting it into a pretend enemy. "Who would ever stand there and let me stab him with a flimsy spear?"

"I agree, probably no one, but you shouldn't criticize the school." I heard Mama call me from the kitchen. Earlier she asked me to get the bathhouse ready while she prepared dinner. I'd already started to heat water, and it was time to fill the tub.

Uncle Hiroshi took the first bath, and in honor of her return, Harumi bathed second. Mama went third, and then me. Sitting on the bench next to the tub, I covered my body with soap and rinsed off quickly. I wanted to soak in the tub while the water was still warm. After working in the field almost all day, relaxing in the bath soothed the muscles in my back and legs. Afterward, since I was the last one to use the water, I drained the tub and cleaned it.

Mama and Harumi had been busy in the kitchen, and by the time I returned to the house, they had our meal ready. Since our dining room floor was covered with *tatami*, we removed our slippers to prevent damage to the mats. The table had been set, and Mama and Harumi carried the food in on trays. The four of us knelt around the table, with Uncle Hiroshi the farthest from the doorway.

Mama had prepared a feast. She served us from a bowl of soba, the noodles and broth fragrant with ginger and green onions. Resting on top, along with the vegetables, was the surprise of our meal— *kamaboka*. I couldn't remember the last time we ate fish cakes—a favorite of mine.

"Mama prepared the cod, but she let me steam it." Harumi's voice reflected her pride. "Do you like it?"

I waited until Uncle Hiroshi picked up his chopsticks and began to slurp the noodle dish. I ate slowly, enjoying every morsel. "This is wonderful, but I'm puzzled. Where did this food come from?"

"Uncle Hiroshi brought it so we could have a special meal," Mama said.

"Yes." Uncle Hiroshi looked up from his bowl. "Gorou Kimura had the good fortune to catch several fish when he took his boat out this morning, and he shared his catch with me. He's also been helping at the market while Maiko is away. He made it possible for me to meet Harumi at the ferry and walk with her."

"That was very kind of him," Mama said. "Please tell him we are grateful for his generosity. There was enough not only for us, but I took some to the little house for Mamoru and Yuriko."

I thought about what Uncle Hiroshi and Mama said. As terrible as our lives had become, people still looked out for each other and shared what little they had. Gorou Kimura was the only young man left in our village. His clubfoot prevented him from fighting. Instead, he spent his time fishing and doing odd jobs. We weren't the only ones who benefitted from his kindness; our overseer and his wife would have a fine meal.

"When does Maiko return from Kyoto?" Mama asked. "You must miss her."

"She returns two days from now." Uncle Hiroshi placed his chopsticks across his bowl as he finished eating, careful to place them so they didn't point to anyone. "I've missed her very much."

"Has her mother recovered from her illness?" Mama gestured to Harumi to clear the table.

Harumi and I carried the dinner trays of dishes to the kitchen and washed them. We worked quickly and returned to the table for a final cup of tea. Mama and Uncle Hiroshi were still talking about Aunty Maiko and her mother.

"I worry about Maiko being gone so long. I think she could have returned sooner. Sometimes I think Maiko's mother enjoys her illnesses and recovers when it's convenient."

"That may be, Hiroshi, but I know that at times it's hard to gauge what a mother or a mother-in-law feels." Mama poured tea for the three of us. "When I married Katsumi and moved into this house, his mother and I had very little to say to each other. Much of the time, I had to guess what she wanted from me, and often I was wrong. Sometimes she would ask me to do little things, just for the attention. Maybe that's what Maiko's mother does."

"Perhaps." Uncle Hiroshi shrugged. "I'll feel better when Maiko's home." He reached for the teapot and filled Mama's cup.

"Mama," Harumi said. "I have a letter for you. From the Kinjos."

"Is there something you need to tell me?" Mama asked her.

"I don't think so." Harumi shook her head. "I don't know what's in the letter."

"Bring it to me," Mama said.

Harumi reached into her pocket and pulled out a crumpled envelope. She handed it to Mama, who pursed her mouth and broke the seal. We waited in silence while Mama read.

"Oh dear," she said as she finished the letter. "Rika Kinjo writes that life in Ginoza has become very difficult." Mama read from the letter. "'Shortages have made it impossible to provide for the family' and 'unfortunately, we are no longer able to have Harumi stay with us.' Harumi, what will I do about school for you?"

"It's all right." Harumi shifted on her knees and leaned toward Mama. "I don't need school. I would much rather stay here and help you and Atsuko."

"But you need school." Uncle Hiroshi joined the conversation. "Education is important."

"Not the education in Ginoza. All we do is practice with st—I mean useless weapons."

"What about math, and writing?" Mama asked.

"I could learn from Atsuko," Harumi said. "She knows more than the teachers I have now."

"That would not be fair to Atsuko," Mama said. "She's already doing the work of a man in the fields."

I was glad to hear Mama speak in my favor. I didn't look forward to teaching Harumi. I loved her, and she learned quickly, but trying to direct her was like attempting to divert the wind.

"But I can help," Harumi said. "I'll work hard, you'll see. I can work in the fields and help take care of the animals. It will be a lot better than attacking straw enemies. *Please* let me stay at home."

"What do you think, Hiroshi?" Mama asked.

"Let's look at both sides," Uncle Hiroshi said. "On one hand, school is the most important part of a young person's life. On the other, Harumi has not seemed to benefit from the government school in Ginoza." Uncle Hiroshi held out his hands palms up as though he were weighing the facts on them. "On one hand, a person could learn manners by living in a city. On the other, Harumi's manners have many holes in them since she's lived away." Again he shifted his hands up and down. "On one hand, the Kinjos have experienced many shortages. On the other, while we have shortages, on a farm, our deficiencies are not as severe." Then Uncle Hiroshi made his last point. "On one hand, Harumi is exposed to rough language and crude behavior in a city filled with soldiers. Here, we can still live with quiet honor." Uncle Hiroshi paused and looked at us with a serious expression.

"What is your decision?" Harumi pressed her hands together.

"I think you should stay here, with your family."

"Good! Wonderful!" Harumi stood and moved forward, as if she intended to hug Uncle Hiroshi in her excitement; then she caught herself and put her hands back together and gave a polite bow. "See, my manners improve already."

"Remember, as soon as I can close my market, Maiko and I will be living here also. It is wise for us to be together." Hiroshi spoke those words to all of us and then turned to Harumi. "Tell me, since your school days may be ended, what was the last lesson you learned?"

"The principal visited our classrooms and read us a letter from the Palace in Tokyo. He said it was from the emperor."

"What was the message?" Mama asked.

"The emperor thinks about all his children. He only wants a distinguished and prosperous life for everyone. The war will bring glory and riches to the entire Japanese empire, and we should feel exalted to choose honor."

"You appear to have learned that lesson," I said.

"It was required," Harumi said. "We recited it over and over while we did defense drills. But I don't understand. If the emperor cares for each of us, and wants us to be prosperous, why don't we have enough to eat, and why are we forced to live by st—silly rules?"

"It's *choosing honor* that troubles me," Uncle Hiroshi said. "People who choose honor have the misfortune of disappearing."

"You mean they *jisatsu suru*?" A chill ran down my spine at the thought of suicide.

"Yes. Maiko wrote me about the Osakas. They were neighbors of her mother, an elderly couple who lost their home, and rather than become a burden, they hung themselves. Maiko thinks they succumbed to pressure to end their lives. I'll be glad when Maiko returns and we can live here—quietly and out of the way."

"Do you have much more to do before you can move here?" Mama asked.

"No. The store's shelves have been mostly empty for a long time, and Gorou will help me pack up the remaining stock. I'll nail the shutters over the windows, but I don't know how much good that will do. The more desperate people become, the more they destroy."

"When you move, you can use Mr. Brave and our cart," Mama said.

"I'll help," Harumi said. "That horse is stubborn, but he'll do anything for me."

"That's very big-hearted of you." I laughed when I said this. "But then, spending time with Mr. Brave is never much of a sacrifice for you."

"It's late, and we have finished our tea. Girls, you can help me clean up. Hiroshi, you know where the *futons* are stored, don't you?" Mama pointed to the hall closet. "You can spread one out in the main room."

The three of us didn't linger in the kitchen after we washed up and put everything away. By the time I reached my bedroom and took my *futon* out of the *tansu,* my eyelids were heavy, and I crawled under the cover, already half-asleep. Hamuri, however, was still full of enthusiasm over the prospect of staying at home.

"I'm so happy. I don't have to go to school—maybe never again. *Yoi*, never again."

"Harumi, I'm tired. I'm glad you're at home, but let's talk about it tomorrow."

"I'll be quiet. Just let me spread my *futon* out." For a few minutes, all I heard was the soft rustle of her bed and its covers.

"You still awake?"

"Barely." I forced myself to remain awake long enough to answer Harumi.

"What do you think happened to the sisters at our old school? Do you think Sister Dominica chose honor?"

"Catholic nuns would never consider ending their lives honorable. To them it's a mortal sin."

"Then what do you think happened to them?"

A terrible pain clenched my stomach in an iron grip. A wave of horror washed over me, as it did whenever I thought about the women who had given their lives to teach us.

"I'm not sure what happened to them, but I'll tell you what I know tomorrow."

Chapter 3

The long slow days of spring,
piling up,
so far away the past.
—Buson

I woke up before Harumi the next day. Her questions about the fate of the Japanese nuns, particularly Sister Dominica, reminded me of the parting gift the young nun gave me before our school closed—a book of Japanese poems. I found the slender leather-bound volume and carried it to the dining room. As I knelt at the table in the early morning light, I looked through the collection of short poems and read the words my teacher wrote on the flyleaf:

> Atsuko,
>   Don't ever lose sight of the beauty that sur-
> rounds us.
>   Yours in Christ,
>   Sister Dominica

Sister Dominica lived those words. A floral arrangement always stood on her desk. Even in the middle of winter when there were no flowers, a vase of bare twigs decorated her workspace. Once, in the middle of class, Sister stopped abruptly; she held her finger up to her mouth, signaling us to be silent. Perched on the sill of an open window, a brown bird with a red belly watched us. It tilted its head toward the room and looked as though it was eavesdropping on our lesson. After a few moments of observing our silent class, the bird flew away with a quick flapping of its wings.

"Mr. Thrush has better tasks to pursue than my history lesson." Sister Dominica laughed softly when she spoke. "Sometimes nature gives us a lesson just as important as any that can be found in books." She paused to let us think about her statement. "What can such a small creature teach us?"

Sayuri raised her hand and stood to share her idea. "Doesn't the Bible say God takes care of all things, such as the lilies of the field and a sparrow that falls from the sky?"

"That's true—good point," said Sister Dominica. "I thought of something else—related to history. People settle disputes by waging battles, and our country is now at war. We fight for land, resources, and control. In the process, many are killed and much is destroyed. What do defenseless birds do when their habitat is lost?" No one said anything, and Sister continued. "The crested ibis has almost reached extinction, but survivors such as the thrush have learned to adapt. These small birds are able to build their nests, raise families, and find food here in the midst of our civilization. In return, we are the beneficiaries of their song and beauty. Something for us to think about—right?"

The day Sister Dominica pointed out the bird visiting our classroom was only a few weeks before our school closed. So much happened since then, and not much was associated with the beauty so vital to our teacher. I sighed and closed my book; telling my little sister about the last days the nuns were on our island would be difficult.

Harumi was awake when I went back to my room to put my book away. "I'm going to the barn," she said as she dressed. "I won't feel like I'm truly home until I say hello to the animals. Are you coming with me?"

"Yes. Today will be a good day to put Mr. Brave and Gentle Lady in the pasture."

"You can lead the cow, I want to take Mr. Brave. He'll be glad to see me."

Harumi found a carrot in the kitchen, and when she held it out to our horse, he neighed a greeting to her. While Mr. Brave munched on the treat, Harumi stood close to his lowered head and silently hugged his neck.

"Do you remember why Papa named him Mr. Brave?" I asked.

"Yes. I was five years old when he was born—old enough to help."

I wasn't surprised that Harumi could recall the winter night when the horse was born; it was memorable. Star, our mare, died giving birth, and the little foal entered a motherless world.

Papa said that the newborn would have to be very brave to face growing up alone and that we would have to be extra careful to make sure he survived.

We fell in love with the little brown horse the moment he was born. Harumi and I used clean straw to wipe him off, and we fed him warm milk from an old baby bottle.

"He likes it!" Harumi said. "Listen to him drink!"

True. Mr. Brave slurped his first meal eagerly. After that night, whenever we were in the barn or out in the field, the colt followed us around. When he saw us with a bottle of milk, he would run toward us on gangly legs, come to an awkward stop, and nudge one of us in the chest.

"Mr. Brave is perfect," Harumi said. "He's the right size."

"For now." Papa laughed. "It won't be very long, and he'll be bigger than Atsuko, and then me. But if you treat him right, he'll always be your *tomodachi*."

"My best friend."

That is exactly what the little *Miyako* horse became—Harumi's best friend. Later, when Papa began to train him, Harumi would hang on the rail of the paddock to watch. Papa spent his entire life around farm animals, and his gentle methods gave us willing servants and lifelong companions. By the time she was ten years old, Harumi could persuade Mr. Brave to back into position between the shafts of the cart and allow her to harness him.

Before Papa died, we had oxen on the farm, as well as more milk cows. Every time he put the oxen to yoke, harnessed a horse, or milked the cows, Papa would thank the creature for being part of the family and helping us. "Our lives would be very limited if we didn't have the benefits of our partners," Papa would say. "It's only correct that we give them our respect and provide a good home."

Sadly, our fortunes changed. Papa's death was only the start of the difficulties. With our country at war, men and supplies became scarce, and Mama was forced to limit our efforts. The result? Smaller fields planted, one horse, one milk cow, and a few scraggly chickens scratching for food in the dirt.

"I see that Mamoru has been here earlier and milked Gentle Lady." I looked over to where Harumi continued murmuring to Mr. Brave. "Are you ready to take him out to the pasture?"

Harumi nodded and turned toward the door of the barn. Leading the horse to pasture was simple; she didn't even need a halter. Mr. Brave followed her the way he had been trained—a few steps behind, walking at her pace. I was next in the little parade. As I led the cow, the bell around her neck jingled our progress.

After we put both animals in the grassy field behind the sheds, they stood still for a few moments and watched us leave. I looked back just before we were out of sight and saw them, heads lowered and grazing. I sighed. We had fewer animals than a short time ago, but the sight of them always brought a feeling of contentment.

After we ate, Uncle Hiroshi left for town. Mama thanked him again for his gifts of food. Harumi said she was grateful for his help as she held out his shoes for him.

"You brought us Harumi, and now you'll be bringing Maiko back," Mama said.

"I won't be at ease until she's home," Uncle Hiroshi said. "I leave on the ferry tomorrow morning. If I'm lucky, I can catch the boat to Honshu and reach Kyoto by nightfall. I want to leave my mother-in-law's house early enough the next morning so we can be back home by evening. It is not wise to travel after dark, but these days, the boats are unreliable."

"True. Your return will be a relief," Mama said.

"And when we come back, we'll close the market and move here. Until then, take care, sister." Uncle Hiroshi bowed politely before turning to walk down the driveway.

"I'll feel safer when the two of you live here." Mama bowed in response.

The three of us stood on the porch and watched Uncle Hiroshi walk away.

"Atsuko, are you and Harumi ready to plant the peanuts?"

"Yes, Mama." I picked up my outdoor shoes and slipped them on over my stockings, while Harumi did the same. "We still have ground to prepare, but we should be able to finish and plant the peanuts today."

Harumi and I went to the potting shed for the tools, and then walked down the drive to the small peanut field across the road. As I did the day before, we worked over the patch of ground that still needed to be prepared. Unlike the way she usually applied herself, Harumi bent over with her trowel and diligently smoothed the dirt I loosened with my hoe.

"You are digging so cheerfully, you must still be happy to be back home." When my sister gardened with me the last time, she complained about how difficult it was, her back hurt, and she was hungry. "Was school on Okinawa that terrible? It must have been more than the spear practice."

"Yes. School was horrible. Our teacher, Nakada-san, was old and bad-tempered. It wasn't so terrible at first, when our teacher was Arakaki-san. He had to leave for the army, and there were no young men left to teach. So Nakada-san came from Hokkaido to teach us." Harumi took the trowel and jabbed it fiercely into the soil. "He didn't like the people of Okinawa—as though he were superior."

"Why did he look down on you? Were the students disrespectful?"

"No, we were too afraid. He called us Ryuku-pigs and said we smelled like armpits." Harumi pinched her nose to mimic her teacher's actions. "That's not all."

"What else?"

"Teacher was old and walked with a cane. When he became angry with someone, he would lash the person across the arms or legs with his wooden walking stick. More than once, my friend Fumio left school at the end of the day with large welts across his arms. When he came back the next day, they had become bruises."

"What did you do?"

"What could I do? The principal wasn't going to stop Nakada-san. There weren't enough teachers. Besides, Mama paid for me to live with the Kinjo family and go to school. Finally, my fortune changed when I became too big a burden and the Kinjos sent me home."

"I'm glad you're here." I smiled at my younger sister, and she returned the smile. I had been lonely ever since our school closed in October. I needed to work on the farm every day, and that didn't leave me any spare time. It was rare when Sayuri had the chance to visit, as she did the day before, or I had the opportunity to go see her. Mama was good company, as well as Mamoru and Yumiko, but I longed for the companionship of someone closer to my own age.

We finished preparing the soil, and when we walked back to the potting shed, Harumi asked me the question I dreaded.

"What happened to Sister Dominica after I moved to Ginoza? You said you'd tell me."

"I'll tell you what I know. Do you remember when Sister Mary Josephine and Sister Esmelda left?" In the shed, I pried the lid off the tin barrel and lifted out the bag of unroasted peanuts I saved from last year.

"Yes, that was a long time ago." Harumi walked close to me as we returned to the field across the road.

"More than two years ago. They were Americans, and it became unsafe for them to remain in Japan after the war started." With the sack between us, Harumi and I each worked an adjoining row. "Don't bury the seeds too deep." I held up my forefinger and thumb about an inch apart to show her.

"I know," Harumi nodded. "I helped last year. But the nuns. Did they go home to America?"

"I don't know. They left in the middle of the night, and Sister Mary Margaret said if their travel plans worked, they would reach a safe place."

"I remember we prayed for them. But even after they left, we still had school."

Our school did remain open, with the young Japanese nuns working hard to continue teaching us. Then came word in October from the government that Maryknoll Academy had been labeled an enemy to the Japanese Empire and would be shut down. That's when I quit school and Harumi moved in with the Kinjo family on Okinawa.

"You left us in the middle of October, the same week our school closed. The six nuns who were here had plans to return to their families. Five left together when Sister Mary Margaret's father escorted them home to Nagasaki. Sister Dominica didn't leave with them. She was waiting for her brother."

"When did she leave?"

"Her brother didn't arrive in time. One day Sayuri and I were at the Seijitsu Market talking to Uncle Hiroshi when Gorou came in and said that a patrol boat just pulled alongside the ferry dock and soldiers were headed this way." By this time, we finished the first rows and moved over to the next two.

"What did you do?"

"Uncle Hiroshi told us to go upstairs and stay with Aunty Maiko. He said to keep the curtains closed and lock the door."

"So you don't know what happened then?" Harumi sounded disappointed; she wasn't going to learn any more.

"We saw some of it. Aunty Maiko showed us how to peek through the sheer curtains and not be noticed. The leader of the soldiers came into the market. We could hear the mumble of voices as he spoke with Uncle Hiroshi, but we couldn't tell what they said."

"That doesn't sound so bad."

"It was the remaining soldiers who did terrible acts. They stormed into the school.

"They went into the school? Sister Dominica?" Harumi gulped, and her eyes widened.

"Yes. They dragged her out into the street and pushed her back and forth, it was almost as if they tried to play catch with her. Then one of them said, 'Stop. We have something better for her.' He pulled her back into the school, and two other soldiers followed."

"Then what?"

"Gorou went out and tried to stop them. But he was outnumbered. One soldier grabbed him by the arm and yanked him out into the middle of the street—in front of everyone. They mocked him—pointing out how useless he was because of his deformed foot. They said he wasn't a real man. Four soldiers surrounded him, and he had no way of escape. Then one used the bayonet on his rifle to cut away his shirt and pants."

"That's horrible. Why would anyone want to hurt Gorou—he's never been cruel."

"He just stood there, his head bowed, while they sliced. It wasn't only his clothes. Wherever the bayonet slashed, a line of blood appeared on Gorou's body."

"What did poor Gorou do?"

"Nothing. He didn't even say anything. When the three soldiers inside the school dragged Sister Dominica back outside, the soldiers who had been torturing Gorou quit. Gorou picked up his clothes, held them to his body, and limped away."

"Did they slice her with the bayonet too?"

"Maybe. Sister's veil had been removed, and her gray habit was ripped and bloody. She could barely walk. When the leader came outside, she looked up, and I could tell that she had been crying."

"They raped her?" Harumi looked sick.

"I think so. But the leader was angry with his soldiers. He yelled at them for not following his orders. They were supposed to board up the school."

"Is that when they nailed boards across the windows? What happened to Sister Dominica? Did anyone help her?"

"They boarded up the school and put the government notice on it. Then they left on the patrol boat and took Sister Dominica with them."

"Poor Sister Dominica. What a horrible fate. Do you think they killed her?"

"I don't know."

"I feel terrible, but I'm glad nothing bad happened to you."

"Me too." But our family didn't avoid trouble. It arrived a few days later.

Chapter 4

During the week after Harumi and I planted peanuts, we helped Mamoru prepare the tobacco fields. Mamoru harnessed Mr. Brave to the plow, and while he pushed down on the wooden handles, he urged the horse to drag the blades through the soil, loosening up the hard-packed earth. Harumi's job was to lead Mr. Brave along and encourage him when he resisted moving forward. She talked to him the whole time, her voice quiet and low. I followed behind, using a hoe to loosen up the clumps left by the plow. It was slow work; Mr. Brave didn't like pulling, and Mamoru struggled with the plow.

"What do you say to Mr. Brave?" I asked Harumi when we stopped for lunch. "His ears move back and forth the entire time you talk, as if he listens to every word."

"Fairy tales." Harumi laughed. "His favorites are *The Bear Guardian* and *The Tengu's Magic Fan.*"

"You say Mr. Brave understands fairy tales? That's a fairy tale."

"No." Harumi smiled. "He likes the sound of my voice, I don't think he cares what I say. Sometimes I recite lessons from school. Yesterday he learned the names of Japan's prefectures."

"That should be a benefit if he ever decides to see more of our country."

"Don't be silly. Mr. Brave doesn't have a travel permit." We both laughed at the absurd picture of our horse sightseeing.

In early March, our work was interrupted by the arrival of Uncle Hiroshi and Aunty Maiko. After my aunt returned from visiting her mother, she and my uncle closed their market and began to pack their belongings. With the help of Gorou, Uncle Hiroshi boarded up the windows of the Seijitsu Market and secured the door with a heavy beam. While Harumi and I were allowed a reprieve from the fields, Mr. Brave continued to work. Harnessed to the farm cart, he made several trips a day, bringing the contents from the market. We stored everything in one of our empty outbuildings. We were glad to see what Uncle Hiroshi brought from town. The items would be useful: cans of kerosene, candles, bags of rice, dried fruit, cloth, scissors, and paper, among other things.

Next came the belongings from their upstairs apartment. Our aunt and uncle had collected many beautiful treasures, and Aunty Maiko carefully packed them for the short journey to our farm. Aunty Maiko's memorable arrival in the last cart trip became a permanent picture in my mind. Mama and I stood in front of our house and watched Harumi lead Mr. Brave up the driveway. Aunty Maiko perched on the cart's seat, surrounded by the last of her boxes. It wasn't a very sunny day, but she held an unfurled parasol over her head and, with her body half twisted around, steadied a stack of boxes. Even though she wore trousers, with an embroidered jacket and her hair drawn back in a chignon, she appeared as elegant as ever.

Mama and I helped Aunty Maiko and Uncle Hiroshi unload the boxes while Harumi took the empty cart and the horse to the barn. Mama had practically emptied the sitting room so Aunty Maiko and Uncle Hiroshi could have it to themselves. Not all their belongings fit in their room, but an unused alcove across from my bedroom held the rest.

"Aunty Maiko, did you bring your collection of dolls?" Harumi asked as we sat knelt around the table, drinking tea.

"Oh yes," Aunty Maiko answered. "I couldn't bear to leave them behind. Hiroshi and I managed to bring all our most valuable belongings." She turned to Mama. "Arisu, you are generous to share your home with us. We are very appreciative."

"It's good that we have family together," Mama said. "This is now your home."

I had wondered how well Aunty Maiko would fit in with our life on the farm; she was so used to living in an apartment. But I needn't have been concerned. The first full day she was with us, she organized the sitting room into a private space for Uncle Hiroshi and her. The next day she announced it was time for her to learn how to farm and she wanted Mama to teach her.

While Uncle Hiroshi helped with the plowing, Aunty Maiko went with Mama to the barn. Days before, Mama prepared seedbeds in the open-air barn using soil mixed with manure. When the beds were ready, she scattered tobacco seeds over them. The day Aunty Maiko joined her in the barn, Mama was covering the tobacco seedlings with small branches to protect them.

Uncle Hiroshi sent me to the barn to ask Mama how many rows she wanted plowed, and when I walked in, Mama and Aunty Maiko were talking and laughing like girls Harumi's age. It was clear that Aunty Maiko didn't expect any special treatment. Later, when I thought about what I'd seen, I realized that Mama must have been lonely for company, just as I had been. She had Mamoru's wife to help in the house, but Yumiko was old and reserved. As hired help, Yumiko felt she had to keep her place. Even though Mama and Yumiko were always polite, I never heard them talk like friends, or laugh together. Now Mama had a friend.

It was fortunate in another way that my aunt and uncle moved to our farm. Shortly after they arrived, Mamoru and Yumiko left us. They received a letter from their daughter, asking for help. Umeko lived in southern Okinawa, where she and her husband had a small farm. But her husband was in the army, and she was alone, caring for three children. She needed them.

We emptied the small house where Mamoru and Yumiko lived for as long as I could remember and loaded their belongings on the wagon. After we said good-bye to the two people who had been with us for so long and Mama gave them packages of food to take with them, Mr. Brave took them to the ferry for their journey.

Mama asked me to help accompany Mamoru and Yumiko to the ferry, and I was glad she did. It gave me a chance to see Sayuri. Ever since I saw her injury, I had worried about my friend. The trip to the village would allow me to find out if she had recovered from her accident with the ferry's chain. We arrived early for the next boat's departure, and I found my friend sitting on a split log that served as a curb on the ferry dock's ramp. As soon as she saw me, Sayuri stood up and walked quickly toward me.

With a warm smile, she bowed a greeting. "I'm so glad to see you!"

"How are you? I've been worried ever you visited me in the peanut field."

"I'm much better. The soreness left a few days after I saw you, and the bruises disappeared as well. But better than that—we received a letter from Junichi!"

"When did he write? Do you know where he is? Is Nobu still with him?"

"He wrote the letter at the end of December. Imagine, it took more than two months to reach us. Mrs. Higa knew how anxious we were to hear, so the day the letter arrived, she left the post office and ran down to the ferry, waving the envelope at us." Sayuri spoke so quickly she had to stop and catch her breath.

"So, what did your brother write?"

"Not much. Just that he's busy marching. They don't have much time to rest, but his health is fine. He's been moved from his first unit, and even though he's not with Nobu anymore, they see each other as often as possible."

"He's marching?"

"I know, it seems odd for my brothers to be fighting on land when they have spent their entire lives around boats. We think from what he wrote they might be in Burma. He described thick jungle, but not much else, and some of the letter was blocked out."

"What did your parents say?"

"Mama's happy Junichi and Nobu are still alive. I don't think she wants to think beyond that." Sayuri looked down the ramp where her father waved to her. "Oh, it's time for me to work—the ferry will leave in a few minutes."

Burma. I thought about what Sayuri told me as I watched her direct travelers onto the ferry before departure. I was fairly certain marching in Burma wasn't good news, but I hadn't wanted to upset Sayuri by saying anything; she looked so happy at hearing from her brothers. Uncle Hiroshi had talked about Burma not many days earlier. He said the monsoons and mountains made fighting difficult. He also had heard that the British, Chinese, and Americans joined forces in Burma after the Japanese took the capital, Rangoon, that the Allies might drive Japan out of Burma.

I helped Mamoru and Yumiko unload the cart and stow their belongings on the ferry. Then I watched as the boat left the dock to make the five-mile trip across the East China Sea to Okinawa. In the days that followed, I discovered that their departure left a void. I didn't know how much they would be missed until I caught myself thinking things such as, *I'll just ask Mamoru how to do this*, or *does Yumiko know where the jars are?*

Those days in March while we prepared the fields and tended the young plants, by the time we finished eating our evening meal, everyone was so tired we didn't stay up very late. Sometimes I went over lessons with Harumi, but often our efforts were unsuccessful. Exhaustion robbed us of the power to concentrate.

"This is silly!" Harumi threw her history book down on the table. "Who cares what happened in the Edo period?"

"It's an important piece of our history." I tried to reason with my irritable little sister, and it wasn't easy, because I felt the same way.

"All this about the shogunate and three hundred *daimyo*—we don't need to know about military leaders and lords from hundreds of years ago. We have enough problems today."

"I agree—for now. Let's put our books away and go to bed. It's already late."

We spread our *futons* and lay in the dark.

"Tell me," I said. "What story did you teach Mr. Brave today?"

"The one he likes most of all—*The Bear Guardian*."

I wasn't surprised Harumi picked that story. Our father used to tell it to her before bed. Every time he asked her what tale she wanted to hear, she always said *"Bear Guardian."*

I decided to indulge her a little. "Can you tell it to me? I'm not sure I remember it."

"You forgot? Never mind, listen to me.

FRANCES SNYDER

The Bear Guardian

There once was a lumberjack who lived all alone in a small mountain village with his loyal dog, for he had no relatives or family. So he would go up into the mountains alone with his dog to gather firewood, which they would sell in the city to buy rice. One morning when the wood-cutter went into the forest to search for wood, his dog ran ahead, its tail wagging, until he spotted what appeared to be an old man ahead. The dog stopped short of the figure and then ran off into the bushes.

"Hey where are you going?" the lumberjack called to his dog, and then he noticed what he'd thought was an old man was really a bear, and it was moaning piteously. Approaching closer, he saw the bear had an arrow sticking out of it.

"Poor thing," the lumberjack thought. "We ought to help you."

So he took the arrow out of the bear, causing blood to gush forth. The dog ran forward then and started to lick the wound. The lumberjack meanwhile ripped some wormwood from a tree and put it on the bear's wound to make it better.

"Lie quietly, don't move, and the pain should pass soon," the old lumberjack said gently to the bear.

As the old lumberjack predicted, the bear soon recovered with his help. Then loyal, like the dog, the bear almost never left his side, but would help him haul the firewood into town. Soon rumors began to spread about a bear that pulled a cart full of firewood. When the curious people saw the lumberjack coming down out of the mountains, they rushed into the streets to greet him and buy his lumber.

The old lumberjack lived thus with the animals, and they worked together this way for some time, but eventually the old man grew too old and died. The lumberjack was buried in the mountains, and the dog and the bear stayed by his grave. Feeling sorry for them, the people would bring them food, but they wouldn't eat. After some time, the dog passed away as well, leaving the bear alone. Later when people went up to visit the grave of the lumberjack, they couldn't find the bear anywhere. They looked for him, and next to a road that wound up the hill, they saw a large stone they started to believe was the bear. Eventually the villagers believed the bear stone to be the village guardian. So when people passed it, they would bow to it and say, "Hello, Mister Bear, how are you feeling today?" The people also asked the bear for help lifting their carts up the steep hill and believed that the bear spirit would help good people, so that when they had an easy journey up the hill, they would thank the bear rock and leave him offerings and pray to him.

By the time Harumi finished reciting the story, she was almost asleep. I lay awake for a little while longer, thinking about my sister and why she liked that particular fable. Maybe because it reminded her of our father. Maybe because it was an animal story, and she loved animals. Probably it was both reasons. Soon, I drifted off to sleep myself.

Two days after Harumi told me the story of the bear that guarded the village, trouble visited our farm. Mama and Aunty Maiko were in the house, Uncle Hiroshi and Harumi were in the barn, and I was feeding the chickens. I heard a heavy truck on the road. That was unusual; not many cars or trucks came by. I was even more surprised to see the truck turn at our driveway and approach the house. Uncle Hiroshi came out of the barn just as two soldiers climbed down from the cab. By this time, Mama and Aunty Maiko came outside to see what was going on. The five of us formed a little group surrounded by chickens pecking at the ground. The older of the two men handed Uncle Hiroshi a letter.

"We have orders to confiscate livestock," the leader said. "The Imperial Army has been authorized to take all large animals. I understand the Oshiro farm has a horse and a cow. We will be taking them with us today."

Harumi emerged from the barn in time to hear the soldier's plan.

"No!" She ran up to Mama and grabbed her arm. "They can't take Mr. Brave! Tell them!"

"Quiet, Harumi," Mama said. "Let me speak." She looked at the soldier. "Our farm produces a reserved crop. We should be able to keep the work animals."

"We have the official document. It doesn't say anything about a reserved crop. We are taking your animals." He turned to the younger soldier, who so far had said nothing. "Go with him." He pointed to Uncle Hiroshi. "Bring the horse and cow to the truck."

"Let me go to the barn," Harumi said, tears streaming down her face. "I'm the one Mr. Brave loves."

Harumi headed to the barn with Uncle Hiroshi and the young soldier following. Meanwhile, the soldier in charge went to the back of the transport truck and pulled out a ramp and rested one end on the ground. After he had done that, he pulled out a cigarette and, with an impatient gesture, lit it.

A few minutes later, Harumi led Mr. Brave out of the barn and toward the truck. Between her sobs, she talked to the soldier who walked next to her.

"And he likes carrots," I heard Harumi say. "Every morning before we start to work, I hug him, and he presses his head against the back of my neck."

The young man nodded at Harumi, and as they went past, I saw him give my sister a look of sympathy.

Maybe it won't be so bad for our horse if he'll be the one to take care of him.

"He can be stubborn," Harumi continued. "If you tell him stories, he'll work harder. He's a very smart horse."

Uncle Hiroshi followed behind them, leading Gentle Lady, her bell clanging a mournful song as she trudged toward an uncertain fate.

When the sad parade reached the truck's ramp, Mr. Brave balked, but Harumi convinced him to step into the dark unknown. Gentle Lady walked up the metal incline in her usual docile manner. Then with a loud bang, the soldier forced the ramp back under the truck and slammed the tailgate in place. I could hear Mr. Brave whinny and stomp his feet in fear at the noise. Both sounds increased Harumi's agitation, and as the truck started down our driveway, she ran behind, shouting, "Stay brave! Be good! Don't forget me!" until she couldn't keep up. She stood there for the longest time, staring as the truck disappeared in the distance, leaving a cloud of dust.

Harumi walked back up the driveway. Tears streaked little rivers down her face through the dust that had settled on it. She didn't say a word; she just passed us and went into the house.

Mama walked over to me; her forehead was wrinkled in concern.

"Atsuko, Harumi is suffering over this latest loss. I know I can rely on you to comfort her."

"Yes, Mama." It was all I said, but a tiny flame of resentment flickered inside me. Mama didn't realize how difficult her request was. Harumi and I were very different. Anyone could know what Harumi was feeling. Her words, gestures, and expressions let people understand her emotions. I wasn't like that. I kept many of my feelings to myself, but that didn't mean I didn't care or couldn't be hurt by cruelty. I cared about Mr. Brave and Gentle Lady; my heart was broken when the soldiers took them away. I sighed and went to look for Harumi. I found her sitting on the floor of our bedroom. Pressed against a wall, she had her knees drawn up with her arms crossed over them. Her face rested on her arms, and she didn't look up when I entered the room.

I slid down next to Harumi and pulled her into my arms. She leaned against me and buried her face against my shoulder. She wasn't crying out loud, but her body shook with her pain. We didn't speak for a long time, but finally she sat up and pushed her hair out of her eyes.

"What's going to happen to Mr. Brave? And Gentle Lady?" Harumi asked.

"I don't know."

"You know how Papa raised them. They were part of our family."

"Animals have ways to survive—even without us." I wasn't sure I believed my words, but I wanted to say something to make my little sister feel better.

"Even in the Imperial Army?"

"I hope so."

"But they don't know anything about being warriors."

"Neither did the boys who have had to fight, but they learned. Look at how well Mr. Brave grew up, and he didn't have a mother to teach him."

"He is smart, isn't he?"

"The smartest."

"I'm going to miss him so much!" Harumi collapsed against me once more and sobbed. It reminded me of the bad dreams she had when she was younger. She'd crawl into bed with me, and I held her until she calmed down and fell back asleep. After what seemed like a long time, I pulled my arm away from her and said, "Come on, I think we need to find some warm water so you can wash your face. You'll feel better."

We left the bedroom, and when we reached the kitchen, Mama was there, chopping up vegetables.

"I'm glad you two are here," Mama said. "Our life on the farm isn't going to be the same. We need to decide how we'll manage without the animals."

I heard Harumi gasp at Mama's words, and I grabbed her hand. I didn't want her to break down again.

"Where were you headed?" Mama asked.

"To wash up," I said.

"That's a good idea. Go do that. Then join us in the dining room so we can discuss our future."

"Yes, Mama." Still holding Harumi's hand, I walked with her to the washroom so we could get ready to learn whatever proposal Mama had for the changes coming to our lives.

Chapter 5

Harumi and I returned to the dining room and joined the rest of the family gathered around the table. Uncle Hiroshi knelt at one end with Mama at the other. Mama had some papers in front of her, including a blank tablet.

"We need to consider our changed circumstances," Mama said. "It will be impossible to run the farm as we are accustomed, now that we've lost Mr. Brave and Gentle Lady."

"The plowing is finished," Uncle Hiroshi said. "We can plant the tobacco."

"That's true," Mama said. "But I don't think we need to plant the entire field with tobacco."

"What do you have in mind?" I asked.

"Last winter we were not prepared for all the food shortages, and we suffered. This is a farm. We should be able to prevent that from happening again."

"Aren't you obligated to produce a tobacco crop?" Uncle Hiroshi asked.

"Yes, but we can plant less and still fulfill the terms from the tobacco monopoly." Mama pointed to a document lying on the table. "I've looked over our contracts, and we can safely cut back our plantings without breaking the conditions of this agreement. We can use part of the field to plant food crops. Luckily, it is still early in the season for planting. The difficulty will be finding the seeds."

"Maybe I can be of help," Uncle Hiroshi said. "My merchant's license allows me to use markets that aren't open to everybody. I can go to the farmer's cooperative on Okinawa. I'll go tomorrow. If I have a choice, what seeds should I purchase?"

"I can make a list." Mama pulled the tablet in front of her and picked up a pencil. "Cabbage. We eat it so many ways—fried or in soups and stews. If we pickle the cabbage, we'll have it over the winter. *Daikon* and turnips. We can pickle those too."

Harumi made a face when Mama mentioned turnips—she didn't like them, but I knew she'd be glad if we grew the giant white radish called *daikon*. Mama's hot pot with radish in it was one of Harumi's favorite meals. However, she didn't join our discussion. She had taken a piece of paper from Mama's tablet, picked up a pencil, and began to sketch. She didn't look up at all.

"Does it all have to be vegetables we pickle?" I asked. "How about tomatoes or *goya*?" Tomatoes and melon were my favorites. "I know they don't last long, but I really like them."

"Yes, we can grow those." Mama added them to her list. "We can preserve the tomatoes and enjoy the *goya* while it is fresh."

"Don't forget other root vegetables. We can keep them for a long time," Aunty Maiko said. "Potatoes, sweet potatoes, taro root, carrot, onion, ginger…"

"*Kobocha*—we have to have *kobocha*!" I pointed to Mama's list to make sure she added pumpkin.

"Good idea," Mama said. "They aren't ripe until late autumn, and that will give us fresh food in winter."

"And we'll still celebrate *Touji*, won't we?" I said. Every year we observed the winter solstice with pumpkin and *yuzu*. Eating pumpkin and bathing in water that had the yellow citrus fruit soaking in it kept us healthy for the rest of the winter.

"Yes, and we'll have to rely on our fruit trees," Mama said. "Last year the pear, apple, and *yuzu* trees were quite bountiful. Hopefully, they will be generous again this year." Mama looked down at what she had written. "We have many different vegetables listed here. We should have sufficient food even if we can't obtain seeds for each one."

"I'll look for all of them, but I don't know how many of these I'll be able to purchase," Uncle Hiroshi said. "There are several markets where I can shop."

During our discussion, Harumi remained silent. I looked down to see what she had drawn. Harumi was a good illustrator, and I expected to see a picture of Mr. Brave—she had drawn many pictures of him before. Instead, Harumi had sketched the truck that visited us earlier. The soldier who ordered us to hand over our animals leaned against the vehicle. The way Harumi depicted him was startling; his face reflected cruelty and evil. When my sister noticed me looking at her artwork, she snatched the paper and rose from the table. Without saying anything, she quickly left the room. I looked at Mama, to see if she wanted me to follow Harumi.

She shook her head no. "Let her go. Poor Harumi, she's learning the bitter lesson of living with loss. You've already tried to comfort her. She can be alone tonight with her sadness, but tomorrow she will join the rest of us and work." Mama must have seen my expression because of what she said next. "I don't want to seem unkind, but Harumi will feel better if she stays busy. And everyone needs to contribute."

When Mama spoke of loss, I thought about Papa's death three years before. Mama didn't mourn, or seem to mourn, after Papa died. During the wake, the funeral, and the series of memorials, she did not give way to emotion. Mama was a petite woman and, at first glance, appeared fragile and delicate. That was misleading. Although she was short and slender, Mama had the strength of steel. With Papa dead, she developed even more fortitude. One look at her expression and the determined way she held her shoulders, we knew better than to contradict her.

After Papa's final memorial, she knelt down at the table with Harumi, Mamoru, and me; and we made plans for our future. Just as we made lists of what vegetables to grow, that night two years before, Mama made a list of what we needed to keep the farm going.

As stoic as Mama acted, I knew she missed Papa. His picture stood in the family shrine, and Mama spoke of him often so we could keep his memory fresh. Several times when she didn't know I was near, I heard Mama talking to Papa—telling him about us or asking his advice. Maybe it was her belief in his spirit's presence that gave Mama the strength to run our farm and take care of us.

Uncle Hiroshi planned to leave early the next morning to catch the ferry that would carry him to Okinawa. Even though he and Aunty Maiko were quiet in the morning, I heard them preparing for his departure. Aunty Maiko wanted him to be sure to stay warm enough, have his money safely hidden, and take food to eat. Uncle Hiroshi answered Aunty Maiko in the same tone she used, one that revealed their fondness, even though they scolded each other. I could picture the two of them—Aunty Maiko fussing over Uncle Hiroshi's clothing while he assured his wife that he had everything necessary.

"With luck, I will find someone with a cart," Uncle Hiroshi said. "Perhaps I'll get a ride to Ginoza—their markets are better than the one in Motobu."

"That would be fortunate," Aunty Maiko said. "But if you cannot find a ride, or you encounter some other delay, it would be best if you remain on Okinawa. The Kinjo family will let you stay with them for a night."

"I will stay if the business of buying seeds takes too long. Don't worry."

"A futile wish. You know I'll worry until you are back. But if it becomes late, stay on Okinawa. It's not safe to travel after dark."

I heard Mama join them as they walked down the hall to the entryway, their voices fading. I pulled myself out of bed so that I could say good-bye. After wishing my uncle success, the three of us stood in the doorway and watched him walk down the driveway, turn to the right, and disappear.

"The weather looks as though it will be kind to us, and we can work outside today," Mama said. "Aunty Maiko and I will make breakfast. Wake your sister, and the two of you come eat."

I didn't know what to expect when I went to wake Harumi. The night before, she was already in bed and was turned to the wall by the time I entered the bedroom. When I told her it was time to rise, all she said was, "Yes," in a low, disinterested voice. However, she did leave her bed and, after dressing, came with me to the dining room.

The day before, I gathered nearly a dozen eggs from our chickens, and Mama used part of them in our breakfast. In addition to porridge made from steamed rice, we had *tamagoyaki*—rolled omelets with a little bit of sugar in them. Such a large breakfast was unusual, but it didn't seem very special. Aunty Maiko was quiet, her mind probably traveling with Uncle Hiroshi, and Harumi's silence was suffocating. She kept her head down and ate only a few morsels before asking to be excused.

"Before you leave, this is today's plan," Mama said. "We can prepare the tobacco field and start to transplant the new tobacco. Harumi, you can show Aunty Maiko how to use a tobacco peg. Atsuko will add water and fertilizer, and I will plant the young starts."

"Harumi, all this is very new to me." Aunty Maiko smiled at my downcast sister. "I've never heard of a tobacco peg. I will rely on you to instruct me."

"It's not difficult," Harumi said. "We just have to make holes."

I'd held my breath, not knowing how Harumi would respond to Aunty Maiko, and was relieved when I saw a tiny smile forming in answer to Aunty Maiko's kindness. Hopefully, Harumi's unhappiness would fade. All the times Harumi was reprimanded for her reckless behavior, she seldom lost her cheerful nature. I would have hated to see that change.

"Atsuko, Harumi, you can help me now. If you clean up from breakfast, I'll prepare *bentos* for our lunch." Mama stood, picked up breakfast dishes, and motioned for us to do the same.

While the three of us worked in the kitchen, Aunty Maiko changed from her pajamas to outdoor clothes. Then she and Mama went to the open-air barn to take the tobacco starts out of their cold frames, while Harumi and I walked to the shed for the tools we needed.

"Here, Aunty Maiko, this is a tobacco peg." Harumi held out a piece of wood carved from the knot of a pine.

"This looks fairly simple." Aunty Maiko held the peg and ran her hand over it. "It's shaped like a cow's horn. And it's so smooth."

"Our pegs are very old," Harumi said. "They're ones my grand-father used—more than fifty years ago."

"*Yare*, and now you are going to teach me how to use one."

"We'll do it together," Harumi said.

"Before you leave to make holes, will you help me?" I asked. Without Mr. Brave, I had to use a pushcart to take fertilizer and water to the field to add to the holes before Mama planted the starts. Luckily for me, when Mamoru packed the bags of cured manure earlier in the spring, he only filled them half full. With four sacks of fertilizer and three buckets of water, I was ready to roll the cart out to the edge of the field.

Mama removed the tobacco from their frames and placed them in a large canvas bag she dragged behind her. Aunty Maiko and Harumi led the way, each carrying a bucket of water, while Mama and I followed.

Once we reached the rows of plowed field, Harumi demonstrated how to use a peg to make a home for the transplanted tobacco.

"You push the peg into the dirt on your side of the furrow, and I'll do the same on mine." As she said this, Harumi crouched down and shoved the peg into the softened mound of soil. "Then we move up about two feet and do the same. We do this until we come to the end, and then we start on the next."

"This doesn't look too difficult," Aunty Maiko said.

"Just be sure the hole doesn't collapse," Harumi said. "If it does, press against the dirt so it holds its shape."

The four of us set to work. Harumi and Aunty Maiko went first, I followed with water and fertilizer, and last was Mama, tucking small plants into their new homes.

While we worked, Aunty Maiko started a one-sided conversation, but as the day progressed, Harumi not only began to respond, but she started to volunteer her opinions. Some of those opinions involved her belief in the uselessness of algebra. All my kindhearted aunt said in reply was "*Yare, yare.*"

After lunch, Aunty Maiko told us a fairy tale. It was one I had never heard before—*Rapunzel*. While Harumi was curious about a beautiful young girl caught in a tower, I became intrigued at the image of someone with golden hair so long that it reached the ground. Aunty Maiko didn't finish the story because we were interrupted by rain that started to fall steadily.

"We can stop now," Mama said. "We've done enough fieldwork for the day."

We packed up our equipment and headed to the barn in time to see Gorou walk up the driveway. He carried a bundle wrapped in old newspaper that he set down next to the back door before he walked over to us.

"Let me help you." Gorou motioned me to stop pushing the cart so he could grab the handles.

It had been a struggle for me to shove the cart up the small hill to the barn, and I was surprised to see how easily Gorou moved it to the barn.

"I heard what happened yesterday," he said. "I didn't think the army would take your animals."

"We didn't either." I lowered my voice. "But let's not talk about it—Harumi has been very upset about losing Mr. Brave."

"We're in hard times. We are at the mercy of the government and the Imperial Army."

"True. But we shouldn't talk about that either."

"I have better news." We reached the door; the five of us huddled under the overhang to avoid what had become a steady downpour. Gorou bent over to pick up his bundle. "I had good fortune today fishing. I thought you would enjoy a masu salmon." He handed the parcel to Mama and gave her a short bow.

"Thank you. This is very kind of you," Mama said. "We appreciate your generosity. Would you stay for dinner?"

"No, I better not," Gorou said. "I need to see about my boat."

"Has the government let you keep it?" I asked. "That's fortunate."

"I didn't give them the chance to decide," Gorou said. "I keep it hidden in Iwa Cove and only take it out when no patrol boats are around." Gorou looked around, puzzled. "Where's your uncle? I hoped to speak with him."

"He went to Okinawa this morning," Aunty Maiko said. "I'm worried—he might not get back this evening."

"If he doesn't return by tomorrow evening, I'll go across and see if I can find him," Gorou said.

"He was going to try to get to Ginoza," Mama said. "He wanted to shop at the markets there, and if he was delayed, he was going to stay with the Kinjo family."

"Will it be safe for your boat if you take it to Okinawa?" I asked.

"I won't take it." Gorou smiled. "The ferry will be good enough for me. But now I must go—with this rain I want to secure my boat in a place where the wrong eyes won't see it." After a short bow, Gorou shuffled down the driveway.

"I'm not going to cook Gorou's fish tonight," Mama said. "We'll have it tomorrow to celebrate Hiroshi's successful quest for seeds."

I was glad when Mama said that; with Uncle Hiroshi still gone, I didn't have much appetite. Instead we had a plain dinner of steamed rice and fried eggs with garlic chives.

The afternoon grew darker with the increasing rain and became a gloomy evening, and the evening seemed to stretch on forever. The four of us sat in our sitting room—now my aunt and uncle's bedroom—and talked about everything except what was on our minds. Finally, it was time for bed. I didn't fall asleep very quickly; the hammering of the rain on the roof sounded as though it was repeating bad news, over and over.

The rain continued the next day. It would be useless to work in the fields. The only chore I did outside all day was feed the chickens. Poor birds, they looked so sad, huddled together in the barn.

In late afternoon the four of us gathered around the table to have tea. By now Aunty Maiko was frantic with worry. She began to describe horrifying predicaments she imagined for Uncle Hiroshi. We tried, unconvincingly, to calm her down.

"He must have been delayed by the weather," Mama set the empty teapot and cups on a tray to carry to the kitchen.

"That's right," I said. "And the ferry is unreliable and never on schedule."

The long dreary day dragged by slowly, and it became even more difficult to distract my aunt from her worries. Finally, when it had begun to grow dark and Mama was about to start dinner, a loud thumping on the door reverberated through the house.

"Let us in! We are about to drown!" Uncle Hiroshi's voice shouted to us.

Mama opened the door, and two men, covered head to foot in drenched clothing, stood on the porch. Aunty Maiko ran to Uncle Hiroshi and, in an untypical fashion, embraced him.

"Let me inside," Uncle Hiroshi said, laughing. "Gorou would like to escape this weather."

"Yes, and I'm not the only one who needs to come in," Gorou said. "Where's Harumi?"

"Here I am." Harumi stepped out from behind me. "What is it?"

"I was walking along the gulch to Iwa Cove, and I heard a voice yelling at me." Gorou put his hand in his pocket. "This little lady insisted I pick her up. I think she needs a home." Gorou handed a little ball of fluff to Harumi. "Would you like to have her?"

"A kitten! A kitten for me?" Harumi looked down at the small creature that meowed loudly while being held. She turned to Mama. "Can I keep her? I'll take good care of her. I'm good with animals. Please?"

"For such a tiny girl, she certainly has a healthy voice." Mama smiled. "I think she is ordering us to keep her."

"Does that mean yes?" Harumi beamed. It was the first real smile I'd seen since the soldiers took Mr. Brave. She stroked the small ball of fur, and the little cat snuggled against her body and started to purr. "She's loud enough to sing in the opera. I'm going to call her Miss Singer." Harumi looked at Gorou, still smiling. "Something wonderful from such a terrible storm—thank you!"

"Hey, what about us?" Uncle Hiroshi laughed. "Does anyone want to hear about my adventures on Okinawa?"

Chapter 6

We gathered around Uncle Hiroshi and Gorou while they removed their rain-drenched coats and hung them on pegs. Aunty Maiko continued to fuss over Uncle Hiroshi, and after he changed his shoes for house slippers, she led him to their room so he could put on dry clothes.

"Gorou, would you like to change into dry clothes?" Mama asked. "I can probably find something that will fit."

"Thank you, but I'm fine," Gorou said. "See, my fishing slicker has kept me mostly dry. I have been in worse weather before and avoided a total soaking." He placed his soggy shoes on the bench near the door while I handed him slippers. "I'm as good as new. I even managed to keep our little friend protected from the downpour." Gorou nodded toward the kitten stirring in Harumi's arms. "Miss Singer has been confined in my pocket too long. Now she's ready to play."

"Stop!" Harumi yelped as the kitten twisted out of her arms and ran into the dining room. Harumi and I followed the cat and found her hunched under the table, meowing loudly.

"Miss Singer is a good name for her. She has a strong voice." Harumi turned to me. "Try to get her to come out from under the table. I'm going to find something we can use as a toy." She walked down the hall to our bedroom.

"The cat will be safe under the table until Harumi convinces it to move," Mama said. "Will you help me with dinner?" It was one of the questions Mama often asked—the kind where there is only one answer.

55

"Yes, Mama," I said. "What do you want me to do?" This time I didn't mind the fact there was only one acceptable reply. Tonight we'd have a celebration dinner. Uncle Hiroshi returned safely, Gorou brought a new pet into our lives, and we would hear the story of our uncle's adventure.

In a short time, Mama and I prepared a dinner Uncle Hiroshi said was "good enough for the emperor and all his ministers." Mama was expert at turning a few ingredients into a delicious meal. This time she used sake, soy sauce, a little brown sugar and combined them for a sauce to use over the salmon that Gorou brought us the day before. While she was fixing the salmon, I made rice and steamed carrots.

Before Mama glazed the salmon, she cut off a little piece and put it on a small plate. "We are not the only ones celebrating tonight. This will welcome Miss Singer to our family."

When we carried the meal into the dining room, we found the others being entertained by Harumi and the cat. Harumi tied knots in an old sock and attached a length of twine to it. When she dangled it in front of Miss Singer, the kitten attacked with both front paws, leapt at the bobbing sock, and rolled back into a ball of fallen kitten. Play ended when Mama and I set the meal on the table and the small plate of salmon on the floor. Miss Singer lost all interest in the sock enemy, rushed over to her first meal at our house, and began nibbling on the fish.

"Hiroshi, you and Gorou must be as hungry as our new friend, let's start," Mama said. "Maiko, will you pour tea?"

Maiko, all smiles, poured tea into the cups of everyone else, and when she finished, I picked up the teapot and filled her cup.

Dinner was festive. The suffocating dread that had hung over our house for the past few days evaporated, replaced by relief at Uncle Hiroshi's safe return and gratitude for the kindness of Gorou. It was evident by the way we laughed at the smallest attempt at humor over silly topics. Aunty Maiko spoke very little, but her quiet smile expressed her joy more than anything she could say. It wasn't until Uncle Hiroshi had his second cup of tea and leaned back from the table, that he told us about his trip to Okinawa.

"It was quite an adventure," he said. "Okinawa has changed—changed a lot."

"Did you reach Ginoza?" Mama asked.

"Yes. I met up with Fumio Nomura, a merchant I know. He gave me a ride to the city."

"Did you go to the Kinjo house?" Harumi asked. "How are they?"

"The house is empty," Uncle Hiroshi said. "I talked with a neighbor. No one knows where they are. I didn't want to ask too many questions. People are apprehensive and don't want to say much."

"Why?" Mama asked.

"The military are everywhere, and no one wants to call attention to themselves."

"That's what I feared," Aunty Maiko said. "I was afraid they would take you."

"The Imperial Army doesn't want an old man like me." Uncle Hiroshi gave a short laugh.

"You are not old—not yet fifty," Mama said.

"You tell me how old I am." Uncle Hiroshi stood up, and as we watched, he transformed himself into a much older man. With hunched shoulders, he clutched an imaginary stick and limped across the room in a painful shuffle. "I pulled my hat down, and of course, I used a real stick. It wobbled because my hands shook."

"What a wonderful disguise." I admired my uncle for his cleverness.

"Remember when I said it was better to be invisible? No one scrutinizes an old man who struggles to walk a few blocks. People look away out of pity, or they are so concerned for their own safety, they cannot be bothered. And men in power have no use for the elderly."

"Did you go to the wholesale markets?" Mama asked. "What about the seeds?"

"I discovered that the wholesale markets have closed. Instead, the space they once occupied is now a training ground for infantry troops. I tell you, when I learned this, I stayed away."

"So you weren't able to buy seeds?" Mama's lowered voice reflected her disappointment.

"Not quite true," Uncle Hiroshi said. "I found another source of good fortune. Fumio Nomura gave me the name of someone to contact. He wrote down the directions to his place of business and included a short note of introduction."

"Was he able to help you?" Aunty Maiko asked. "What is his name? How can we thank him?"

"I don't think he wants to be thanked," Uncle Hiroshi said. "He's not in business for kindness—he likes money. His name is *Hayai-san.*"

"His name is Mr. Quick?" Harumi wrinkled her nose. "I never heard a name like that—is he Japanese?"

"I don't think that's his real name," I said. I'd heard about the black market, and now it appeared as though our family was part of it.

"I did not ask Mr. Quick any personal questions," Uncle Hiroshi said. "I didn't think it would be very healthy. After all, he thought he was dealing with an old man from the countryside."

"Did he sell you seeds?" Mama asked.

"Not immediately. I met him in a small house that faced a narrow alley. He had no merchandise there. He gave me a slip of paper with his name on it and instructed me to go to an abandoned garage on the outskirts of town. I was to give it to *Osoi*, the man who guarded the garage."

"Mr. Quick's partner is named *Slow*?" Harumi started to laugh.

Uncle Hiroshi looked at Harumi briefly. "Niece, would you go to the entryway and bring the two packages I left there?" As Harumi left the dining room, Uncle Hiroshi turned to the rest of us. "When it started to rain, I was glad I had thought to bring oilskin bags. Otherwise, my purchases would be ruined."

Harumi returned with the two waterproof satchels, one much bulkier than the other. She set them down next to Uncle Hiroshi, and he grabbed the smaller one. After untying the bindings, he tipped it over the table, and seed packets tumbled out.

"Hiroshi—what a wonderful collection you bought!" Mama said. "We will have an excellent garden."

We shuffled through the pile, exclaiming over all the different seeds that Uncle Hiroshi bought from Mr. Quick and Slow. Tomatoes, melons, daikon, carrots, and pumpkin, among others.

"Harumi, I'm sorry to disappoint you," said Uncle Hiroshi, "but I wasn't able to find any turnip seeds."

"Yes! Tonight just became better than ever," Harumi said. "A new cat, and now no turnips."

"I'm not quite finished," Uncle Hiroshi said. "We haven't looked in the second bag." He lifted the bulky oilskin bag to the table and, after untying it, pulled out a boxlike item made of wood. On one side were dials and a wire that was attached to a curved metal band with discs on each end.

"It's a radio," Uncle Hiroshi said. "Now we can listen to the news, or anything else broadcast over radio waves."

"But we don't have electricity." Mama shook her head.

"It doesn't matter," Uncle Hiroshi said. "This is a wireless radio."

"But there's a wire, right here." Harumi touched the short wire attached to the front of the box.

"No, *wireless* means it doesn't use electricity. This is a crystal radio. I tested it. It's old, but it works fine. Let me show you." Uncle Hiroshi placed the band over his head so the discs at each end covered his ears. "These are earphones—the sound comes through them. I'm going to turn the dials until I hear something. *Osoi* said that the main station from Tokyo, JOAK, is 590." Uncle Hiroshi twisted the dial that pointed to a series of numbers to the left. After moving the knob slowly while he listened, Uncle Hiroshi stopped and smiled. "I have a station. I hear voices."

Everyone took turns passing the earphones around so we could hear what someone said over radio waves many miles away. When it was my turn to listen, the sound wasn't very clear—scratchy noises interfered, along with voices from other stations, but it was like magic nevertheless. For those of us who lived on the small island of Iejima and only received mail a few times a week, and a government-run newspaper even less often, the radio made an exciting difference in our lives. Even though many of the broadcasts were propaganda, they became our "ear to the world."

That night, with the return of Uncle Hiroshi and Gorou and time spent listening to the wireless, it was late by the time the evening broke up. Mama told Gorou it was too late for him to go back to town.

"The storm continues, and you have a long walk in the dark. Mamoru's house is empty since he and Yumiko left for their daughter's home. There is no reason you can't stay there." Mama turned to me. "There is an extra lantern in the kitchen. Please fill it for Gorou."

After putting kerosene in the lantern, I took it to Gorou, who was in the entryway, fastening the clasps on his slicker.

"Do you know which building is Mamoru's?" I asked.

"Yes, it's left of the barn where Mr. Brave and Gentle Lady used to stay."

"Right. It's a small house. Only a main room and a sleeping room. You can find a futon in the closet. Will you be here for breakfast?"

"Thank your mother for letting me stay, but I'll be gone before breakfast. I need to check my boat. I left it secure, but I want to make sure it wasn't damaged in the storm."

"You'll be okay?"

"Don't worry about me." Gorou smiled and briefly touched my arm. "I've been looking after myself for a long time." Then he turned and walked out the door, closing it behind him.

In the kitchen, Mama and Aunty Maiko washed the dishes I brought in from the dining room. While they worked, I straightened up the dining room, wiped the table, and returned to the kitchen. Meanwhile, Harumi made a bed for Miss Singer; she folded an old towel and placed it in a wooden box that stood next to the stove. The only thing missing from the kitten's bed was Miss Singer. Every time Harumi put her down on the towel and removed her hand, the kitten jumped up, rubbed against Harumi's leg, and meowed. If Harumi walked away, the kitten went with her, as if she were glued to Harumi. Of course, Harumi didn't seem very sad that Miss Singer had become so devoted.

"Harumi, take the cat's bed to your room," Mama said. "Please don't tell me if Miss Singer decides not to stay in it, but sleeps with you instead. I don't want to know. More than that, I don't want her 'singing' all night."

"Yes, Mama." Harumi picked up the box and, with Miss Singer following close behind, left the kitchen.

"Did Uncle Hiroshi go to bed already?" I asked. Usually he was the last one up and liked to check the doors and windows before turning in.

"He was exhausted," Aunty Maiko. "He's not an old man yet, but his trip to Okinawa tired him out. Poor Hiroshi, he's never shopped in the black market before. So many changes for him— becoming a farmer and now dealing with scoundrels."

"We all need to get to bed," Mama said. "If the weather lets us, we have a lot to do tomorrow. I'm worried about the tobacco we've put in the ground, and there are more to plant, along with all the seeds Hiroshi bought." She sighed. "Work on a farm never stops, even in the middle of a war."

The rain stopped early in the morning. By the time we ate breakfast and went outside, pale sunlight shone through the clouds as they broke apart and drifted away. Out in the field, the young tobacco plants looked like defeated soldiers as they drooped over the furrows, beaten down by the relentless rain the day before.

"What do we do now?" Aunty Maiko asked. "After all our hard work."

"This isn't so bad." Mama held herself upright and squared her shoulders. "We can save most of these plants. They're young, and if the roots haven't been damaged, we can replant them. If not, fortunately we have more starts than we need." Mama motioned to me. "Atsuko, please go to the shed and bring out the tools we used yesterday."

When I returned with the pushcart holding implements and a barrel, Mama organized us into a work party. Harumi and Aunty Maiko worked together—carefully removing the tobacco starts and setting them aside for Mama to inspect. I reworked the holes, mixing dry soil from the barn with the wet, making them able to hold plants again. Mama had Uncle Hiroshi work with her, showing him the way we planted tobacco and how to tell which plants were in good enough shape to be replanted.

We had been working for over an hour, when I heard my name. It was Gorou. His arrival was a surprise. I thought he would be out on his boat.

"Hello," I said as I walked to meet him. "I didn't expect to see you today."

"I didn't think I'd be back so soon, but Sayuri asked me to bring you this." Gorou handed me an envelope.

"From Sayuri?" I was puzzled. It seemed odd that she would have Gorou deliver a letter to me. When we wrote to each other, we usually just left the notes in our postboxes. But we didn't write often. I broke the seal and removed a single sheet from the envelope and looked at the brief message.

"Oh no!" I felt as though someone punched me in the chest. I read the note again, hoping I had been mistaken the first time.

"What's wrong?" Gorou asked. "You look sick."

Harumi had heard me and came over. "Are you all right?"

"No, I'm not all right." I pressed the letter to my body. "Sayuri is leaving Iejima."

"What? Why?" Harumi asked.

"Her father has been removed from his job as ferry captain. They have to leave their house."

"That's horrible!" Harumi stomped her foot. "How can they do this? It's not right."

I remembered what Uncle Hiroshi said about people who were encouraged to choose honor and how they disappeared. Was that going to happen to my best friend?

Chapter 7

"Will you wait a few minutes?" I asked Gorou. "I need to write back to Sayuri." I ran back to where Mama and Uncle Hiroshi worked setting out young plants and told them the news about Sayuri's family.

"The family has to relocate in two weeks. She wants to see me before they leave," I said. "She has a gift for me, and I'd like to give her one in return. I need to let her know we can meet." I ran to the house, found pencil and paper in my portable desk, and wrote a short reply. As she suggested, I responded that a short visit on Saturday—two days away—was agreeable. She could come and spend the afternoon with me.

Later that evening, I looked through the chest in my bedroom. I had decided earlier what I wanted to give Sayuri. Underneath my school uniform, I found the small box I kept there. My pearl.

When I was ten years old, I did much of the work in the peanut field. I helped prepare the furrows and then weeded and watered the growing plants. I even went with Papa to Okinawa and sold the peanuts at the market. Papa said that because I worked so hard, I could keep a portion of the money.

Not long afterward, my family went to Kyoto to visit Uncle Hiroshi and Aunty Maiko. While there, Papa took me to Toba, a city on Ise Bay where women dove for pearls. I was fascinated by everything I saw. The fishermen's wharf on our island wasn't like the seafront in Toba. Our pier handled the business of fishing—boats, nets, floats, and most of all, fish. The dock at Toba didn't have any of that. Toba's trade involved the many tourists who clustered around the booths. For a fee, a diver would plunge into the water and bring up an oyster or mussel. If a pearl was found inside the shell, it became the property of whoever paid the fee.

I was in awe at the idea of finding pearls, and even more amazed by the *ama* who dove. Their diving costumes startled me—sheer white loincloths that became sheerer when wet. Every time a woman plummeted, I would hold my breath as if I were the one underwater. Of course, I couldn't go without breathing for even a minute, and I exhaled when it became painful. The diver always stayed under long after I gasped for air. Some of the divers spent five minutes searching for oysters. Papa told me that they could go down as far as a hundred feet, which seemed astonishing to me.

I asked Papa if I could buy a chance, and he nodded. I purchased a ticket and selected one of the women to dive for me. I was disappointed at first because she didn't stay under very long, but to my joy, when the oyster was opened, it held a pearl.

Papa was as happy as I at my good fortune, and he paid for a setting to be attached to the pearl and a silver chain so I could wear it around my neck. I proudly wore the necklace whenever I dressed up, but now that I spent most of my time working in the fields, I kept my pearl tucked away.

I looked down at the jewel in my hand, rubbing it softly. It was very precious to me, but I thought back on what Papa once told me about the things we treasure. He said the value is in the memories, not the item itself. If I gave my most prized possession to Sayuri, the pearl would keep our friendship alive.

The thoughts that tore through my brain kept me from sleeping that night. Long after the house became silent, I stayed awake and considered how important Sayuri was to me, and how much I treasured her friendship.

We met as four-year-olds. Both of us started school the same day. Dressed in our uniforms, we had leather packs on our backs and carried *bentos* in our hands.

"You're Atsuko, aren't you?" Sayuri asked.

"Yes, and you're Sayuri," I said. "I know who your father is—he runs the ferry. I live on a farm."

"I know," Sayuri said. "Do you know what we're supposed to do?"

"Mama told me that we go inside when a bell rings." That was the simple way I met my best friend. When a bell rang and everyone ran to the school's entrance, Sayuri and I joined hands and climbed the stairs to Maryknoll Academy for our first day of school. By the time the school year was over, we were experienced students and moved beyond preschool and into first grade—still best friends.

Now what will happen to Sayuri? All I could think of was what Uncle Hiroshi said about people disappearing. But I didn't know the reason Sayuri's family had to leave, or why her father lost his job. Maybe they weren't going to "disappear." Then a wicked little demon would whisper, "It could be worse—you never know." *Not Sayuri, not Sayuri, not Sayuri…*went through my mind, over and over, until finally, I fell asleep.

Saturday, Mama told me that I didn't need to work after lunch; Sayuri and I could spend the whole afternoon together. However, she didn't want Sayuri to walk home when it was dark, so she should leave when there was still an hour of daylight left.

Soon after eating my midday meal, I changed my clothes, took the package I wrapped in red-colored paper, and walked down the driveway to meet my friend. Sayuri and I had been meeting each other partway ever since we were old enough to visit on our own. Sometimes we met at the edge of the woods, where we could sit on an old moss-covered log. One, or both of us, would bring treats; and we ate them without the interference of Harumi, who sometimes pestered us.

When it was time for us to go home, we had a ritual of both walking together a short way—back and forth and back and forth—until it became so late we needed to run home to avoid being gone too long. That was before our lives became difficult, when Sayuri and I spent time together without fear and anxiety hovering over us. However, our lives had changed drastically; that Saturday we didn't talk as had so many times before, where we spent the afternoon discussing our far-fetched plans, or giggle about which boy in class was the best-looking. With Sayuri's departure looming, I wanted to say all the important things a person says when it might be the last opportunity to talk with a friend.

I walked around the curve in the road not far from where the woods began and saw Sayuri waiting for me. She sat on the log covered with a cushion of moss. When she caught sight of me, she jumped up and ran toward me. We met, briefly hugged, joined hands, and walked back to the log. It reminded me of the time we walked into school together, more than twelve years earlier.

"What happened?" I asked. "Why do you have to leave?"

"Papa received a letter three days ago," Sayuri said. "He is no longer in charge of the ferry. The military will be running it from now on."

"Can't you stay on Iejima anyway? You have a house here."

"It's not our house. It belongs to the ferry service. That means it belongs to the government."

"Where will you go?"

"We could go live in a camp."

"Is that what you'll do?"

"Papa said we aren't required to live at the camp. He wants us to go to Naha and live with my grandmother."

"That will probably be better than living in a camp."

"Maybe. My grandmother is a difficult woman, and her husband is a strange man."

"Uncle Hiroshi said the camps were not organized, and people struggled to obtain enough food." I didn't tell Sayuri some of the other things Uncle Hiroshi told us about the conditions—besides terrible food shortages, water and fuel were scarce. Many people had to use the same toilet. I kept these thoughts to myself. Sayuri was already frightened without knowing how horrible her life might become.

"Let's talk about something else," Sayuri said. "I have a present for you. Here." She handed me a small package wrapped in gold foil.

"Thank you. And I have a gift for you also." I gave her the small box wrapped in red paper. I carefully removed the paper from the package Sayuri gave me. "Oh! What a wonderful present!" I lifted a small elephant from the wrapping and held it up. It had been cut from jade. Even though it was not very big, the elephant's features were distinct. One of its forelegs was bent to show it was walking, and the trunk curled back on itself as if the animal trumpeted its presence. A loop on its back had been threaded with a pale-green ribbon.

"It's flat," Sayuri said. "If you wear it around your neck, it'll lie snug against your chest. Papa told me elephants represent wisdom and longevity. I hope this one gives you those qualities."

"It's perfect." I lifted the ribbon over my head and adjusted the elephant's position. Even in my plain shirt, I felt elegant with the beautiful little carving lying over the rough cotton. "Open yours." I was eager for Sayuri to have the gift.

"Your pearl!" Sayuri opened the small box and took out the necklace. "You're giving me your pearl? Your precious pearl?"

"Yes, I want you to have it," I said. "With you, the pearl will be even more valuable."

"I'll keep it always! Thank you."

We sat on the old log for a long time. At first, we didn't talk about anything important, as I'd thought we would. Maybe the very ordinary topics were safe ways for us to express our feelings, without actually speaking them.

"Do you remember Riko and Sora?" Sayuri asked about two girls who had been in our class several years before.

"Yes—but they weren't friends of ours." I didn't know why Sayuri mentioned them. We hadn't spent much time with either one.

"They were silly, weren't they?"

"I remember Sister Mary Josephine calling them that," I said.

"Their friendship baffled me. At times they acted as though they were glued together and couldn't be separated. Sora even finished Riko's sentences for her, and they had to wear matching clothes."

"I was glad that we weren't like that." I shook my head. "I wouldn't like it if we lived on top of each other."

"Well, I was thinking about what happened when we were in lower secondary."

"Do you mean the fight?"

"Yes."

It was an embarrassing event, and happened during lunch one day, but I never found out why those two had such an unpleasant disagreement. I was with the girls in my class, sitting around a table outside when Riko and Sora began to argue. It didn't end with their harsh words, however. Sora grabbed Riko's lunch, threw it on the ground, and stomped on it. Riko snatched at Sora's jacket and ripped off the breast pocket. They were about to pull each other's hair when Sister Mary Josephine stepped between them. She grabbed both girls by the arm and marched them into the school building. I never saw either girl again. I think their parents moved them to a school on Okinawa. Wild stories spread; one was that they had run away to Tokyo and lived on the streets. I never believed that rumor; nevertheless, I was relieved when they left our school.

"Why are you thinking about those two?" I asked.

"Two reasons. They went away, and we didn't see them again. Like what might happen to me. The other reason, I was thinking about our friendship. We've never fought. I never even wanted to fight. Did you?"

"No. We've had disagreements, but never to the point of anger. I'm glad."

"Me too."

As the afternoon approached evening, our conversation became more serious.

"Sayuri, what do you want to do? I mean after the war, when you return?"

"I want to work at the job I've always wanted—to be a book-keeper for my uncle. What about you?"

"My dream is still to go to university and study literature, but everything has changed. I don't think it will be possible anymore."

"Let's make a pact!" Sayuri held out her hand. "We promise each other that when the war is over, we find each other and pursue our dreams. Do you agree?"

"Yes." I reached for Sayuri's outstretched hand and solemnly shook it. "I have no doubt we will meet again, here, on Iejima."

The daylight began to fade, and just as we had done so many times before, Sayuri and I walked each other back and forth until we were in danger of being caught by darkness. With one last hug and promises we would write, we parted. I stood in the road and watched her walk away; she rounded a curve, and was gone.

After dinner, Harumi and I knelt at the table. I read while Harumi bent over the paper in front of her and concentrated on the essay I suggested she write. In the background, I heard the soft murmurs of Aunty Maiko and Uncle Hiroshi as they talked in their room. Mama worked in the kitchen, stopping to scold the kitten singing for her supper. Ordinary sounds made by a family at home, pursuing their usual activities. I sighed and looked down at my book, searching for the words to express how I felt. Most of the poems were love poems, and I wondered if Sister Dominica knew that when she gave me the book. I did find two that mirrored my thoughts and copied them down in my best handwriting.

> *My keepsake—*
> *Look at it and think of me,*
> *and I will remember you*
> *through the long years*
> *strung out like beads on a string.*
> *(Lady Kasa)*

> *As Mount Arima*
> *Sends its rustling winds across*
> *The bamboo plains*
> *I will be just as steadfast*
> *And never forget you.*
> *(Lady Kataiko)*

Harumi looked up from her paper and asked me, "Do you think Mr. Brave will ever come back?" Her mind clearly wandered from the essay topic—an explanation of Japan's parliament.

"I don't know," I said. I believed that we would never see our horse again, but didn't want to put that thought in Harumi's head.

"You two better finish what you are doing." Mama came out of the kitchen, followed by Miss Singer. "I don't want to use up kerosene. It's so difficult to find."

"Everything is terrible." Harumi threw her pencil down on the table. "We lose our animals. There's not enough kerosene. Why is war so hard? I thought it was supposed to make our lives better. That's what they told us at school."

"That was the idea." Uncle Hiroshi joined us in the dining room. "But war is a hungry beast and demands to be fed. It eats everything Japan can give and asks for more."

"This year it will be different," Mama said. "Our plans will out-fox the beast. Come, let's go to bed."

Later, I thought about what Mama said. *Without her optimism, could we survive?*

Chapter 8

By late April, our farm had changed from the empty brown fields of March to rows of young green plants, promising us food for the coming year. It appeared as though Mama's plan and Uncle Hiroshi's business with the black market were successful. Of course, we still needed to care for the crops as they grew and harvest them when they reached maturity.

On a warm May morning, Aunty Maiko, Harumi, and I set out to tend the peanut field. Harumi, followed by Miss Singer, went to the toolshed for hoes and trowels, while Aunty Maiko put together our lunch. I pumped water from the well into two buckets and carried them across the road. Uncle Hiroshi followed me with more water and brought it down for us in the pushcart. Then he left to join Mama; they were going to work with the carrots and *daikon*.

"Atsuko, you and Harumi will have to explain peanut farming," Aunty Maiko said. "I've never grown them before. Is it similar to what your mama showed me with the tobacco plants?"

"A little the same," I said. "We inspect the plants to see if they are healthy and then look to see if we need to thin them—just as we did with others." I showed Aunty Maiko how to know which ones needed to be pulled. "They should be at least ten inches apart. If you need to remove plants, pick the ones that look the least healthy." We started at the first row, and I showed Aunty Maiko what to look for—withered leaves and signs of being eaten.

Harumi, who had worked with me in the peanut field the last several years, started on the row next to us; however, Miss Singer wove herself around Harumi's arms and legs, interrupting her progress. While Harumi made her way down the row, she attempted to entertain the cat with the story of "The Boy Who Drew Cats." Miss Singer meowed her approval of Harumi's story about magical cats that saved the day. Of course, Miss Singer gave us her opinion any time we talked to her.

"Oh, look," Aunty Maiko said. "Near the bottom—little yellow flowers. Do we snap them off the way your mama told me to do with the tobacco?"

"No." I held my hand out to stop her. "If we remove the flowers, we won't have any peanuts." I handed her a trowel and grabbed one for myself. "First, I loosen the dirt around the roots." I put down my trowel and picked up a bucket. "Next, water. They need enough to drink, but not be waterlogged." I poured water around the base of the plants.

"Like this?" Aunty Maiko carefully dug around a plant. "Why don't we snip the flowers?"

"Look at this." I pointed to where the petals were beginning to fall off a bloom. "See the short stem growing from the base of the flower?"

"Yes, I see."

"It's called a peg." Then I pointed to the soft earth below. "It grows and arches down until it buries itself in the ground. That's where the peanut develops."

"*Yare*," Aunty Maiko said. "I'll be sure to work carefully. I don't want to destroy any peanuts."

The three of us made our way down the first two rows, Harumi working alone while Aunty Maiko stayed with me—occasionally asking for my opinion on which plants to remove.

After that we each had our own row. Harumi told more stories to Miss Singer while we worked. The tales she told reminded me of Papa. They were ones he used to recite to us at night before we went to sleep. I don't know if they had the cat's attention, but I enjoyed listening to her chatter; and when I glanced over at Aunty Maiko, I saw her small smile of appreciation.

We had been digging and watering for nearly an hour when Aunty Maiko stood, put her hand to the small of her back, and arched forward. "I'm using muscles I've never used before, they're starting to complain."

"You can stop," Harumi said. "Atsuko and I can finish."

"No, I don't want to quit," Aunty Maiko said. "I told your mama I want to learn how to farm, and giving up isn't the way to success. But how about if the three of us work together on the next row and, when we finish, stop for lunch?"

Harumi and I agreed, and in a little while, we finished a row together and put our tools down. I carried the lunch Aunty Maiko made earlier over to the pine tree next to the east side of the field. Harumi spread out a blanket, and the three of us sat down in the shade. Aunty Maiko wasn't the only one needing to rest from crouching over the peanut plants. I was glad to let my cramped muscles relax. At first we didn't talk much; we were too busy eating.

"Peanut plants are very interesting—they are like a woman." Aunty Maiko was the first one to break our silence.

"What do you mean?" Harumi asked. "Lots of other plants have prettier flowers than peanuts."

"I'm not talking about how decorative the flowers are," Aunty Maiko said. "I'm thinking about how the flowers are the attractive parts of plants, the same as what you see on a woman's face is her initial appeal, but just as the peanut grows underground, a woman's true value is within—it's the quality of her character."

"I never thought of that before," I said. "I'm writing it down later."

"Aunty Maiko, how do you do it?" Harumi asked.

"Do what, dear?"

"Be beautiful all the time. You've been digging in the field with us all morning, and you don't look as though you've been working. You're like a *hime*."

"Oh, no." Aunty Maiko laughed. "I'm not a princess at all. Before I met your uncle, I worked for a living. As for how I appear now—look at me—I'm wearing clothes I borrowed from your mama, and my shoes are covered with dirt."

It was true, Aunty Maiko wore work clothes and rough clogs, but she still managed to look elegant. Her hair was always neatly arranged, and the graceful way she held herself gave her dignity.

"Do you remember the day Atsuko and I had tea at your house?" Harumi asked. "I was nervous at first. I didn't know you very well, and you looked so—I don't know—special—in your kimono."

"Oh," Aunty Maiko said. "Your Uncle Hiroshi and I had just moved to Iejima a short while before, so you didn't really know us."

"Why did you come here? To run the Seijitsu Market?"

"After what happened in Kyoto, we were fortunate to be able to buy the market here."

"What happened?" I began to wonder what terrible event forced my aunt and uncle to abandon the city where they once lived.

"You knew your Uncle Hiroshi was a silk merchant, didn't you?" Harumi and I nodded.

"Because of his position with Takahashi Silk Merchants, we traveled the world—selling high-quality silk to leading fashion designers."

"That's when you bought all your dolls," Harumi said.

"Yes, I acquired them in places we visited. We were never wealthy, but we could live as though we were. Then, it ended. In 1935, the company suffered enormous losses, and the business failed. It was our good fortune the Seijitsu Market was available and we were able to buy it. When it became impossible to run the market because of shortages, your mama gave us a home, so our luck has prevailed."

"Sister Mary Josephine told us people make their own luck," I said, "and you and Uncle Hiroshi work hard."

"You said you had a job before marrying Uncle Hiroshi," Harumi said. "What did you do? Were you a silk merchant? How did you meet?"

"*Yare.*" Aunty laughed softly. "It was so long ago. First of all, no, I wasn't a silk merchant. When I was young, women didn't have such positions. But I did have a very good occupation—I was a seamstress. Most seamstresses worked under dreadful conditions—long hours, poor pay, and unsafe buildings. I had it much better. I trained under the great Kazuhiro—the most renowned tailor in Kyoto. Because of my training, I obtained a post with the House of Hisakawa."

"Where you met Uncle Hiroshi!" Harumi waved her arms in excitement.

"Not quite," Aunty Maiko said. "At first I worked in a large room with many other women. Then I was chosen to be a 'beautiful' girl."

"Like a *geisha*?" Harumi's eyes widened.

"No, nothing like that. I still operated a sewing machine, only it was in the front of the building. I sat by a large window, and people on the street could see me, and of course, silk merchants who did business with the company passed by each day."

"It must have been glamorous—being admired and meeting important people," Harumi said.

"Not always." Aunty Maiko hesitated before she continued. "Life in big cities is very different than small places like Iejima."

"It's more exciting," Harumi said.

"That may be. However, sometimes people who think they are important aren't easy to be around." Aunty Maiko's tone was serious.

"What do you mean?" I asked.

"There are strict rules for women to follow." Aunty Maiko spoke slowly. "Women are judged on everything they say or do. The smallest mistake can ruin a woman's future. It's the same with appearance. It is essential that a woman be perfectly groomed." Aunty Maiko spoke slowly. "But men have few restrictions on their behavior."

"That's not right!" Harumi said. "People around here don't act that way."

"No, it's the culture of life in the cities—with people who have money," Aunty Maiko said.

"Doesn't it make marriage difficult?" I thought about Mama and Papa and the respect they gave each other.

"Most Japanese businessmen are married, but very few of them spend much time in their marriages. Wives can be neglected, and that's the problem."

"But Uncle Hiroshi isn't like that!" Again, Harumi raised her voice when she spoke.

75

"No, he isn't," Aunty Maiko said. "That's why I married him."

"Talking about me?" Uncle Hiroshi came up behind us. He had the pushcart with him. "I'll take the empty buckets back and fill them with water."

Uncle Hiroshi's arrival was our signal to go back to work. For the rest of the afternoon, we each worked our own rows and by late afternoon managed to finish the entire field of peanuts.

Spring turned into summer; the days grew warmer and longer. The four of us had adopted a routine: after working outside all day and eating dinner, we gathered in Aunty Maiko's and Uncle Hiroshi's room, taking turns listening to the wireless. The entire family usually spent the evenings together in what had once been our living room. Not only because the radio was there, but if we had to burn kerosene, we only needed it in one room. However, since it was summer, we hardly used any lamp oil. The days stayed light longer, and we were so tired from working all day, nobody had the energy to stay up very late.

One evening in mid-June, Uncle Hiroshi, wearing the headphones, turned the dial on the crystal radio set. "I'm picking up Radio Tokyo."

"What's on?" Harumi asked. Sometimes the broadcast was an entertainment program, and Uncle Hiroshi gave the headphones to her.

"War news," he said.

The government controlled all the radio stations, and frequently the broadcasts were reports from the military.

"A battle in the Philippine Sea—between Saipan and Formosa."

"That's not very far from here," I said. Earlier most of the fighting was far removed from us, places such as Burma, Malaysia, and Singapore. I grabbed the atlas sitting next to the radio and opened it to our part of the world. "The battle's not even four hundred miles away. That explains all the planes flying overhead recently."

"This announcement is coming from the office of Admiral Toyoda," Uncle Hiroshi said. "The fighting is between aircraft carriers."

"Who's winning?" Harumi looked up from where she sat on the floor, playing keep away from the cat with a ribbon.

"The report's not clear." Uncle Hiroshi frowned. "Vice Admiral Ozawa is in charge—they are following the strategy of the Imperial Navy—our warriors are fighting with bravery and honor—we should take pride in the valor of the Japanese." Uncle Hiroshi was quiet for a few minutes while he listened. "Nothing is being said about which side is prevailing. That is not good."

I continued studying the map in the atlas. A few days before, we'd heard reports of fighting in Saipan. Again, the broadcasts didn't tell us which side was victorious. However, our Army and Navy must not have defeated the enemy; otherwise, we wouldn't be fighting in the Philippine Sea.

"That's all the war news—wait—how strange—now someone is speaking English…" Uncle Hiroshi handed me the headphones. "Maybe you can understand what they are saying."

"I'll try." I slipped the headphones over my ears.

Sister Mary Josephine had been teaching English to the older students before she left our school. Even though Sister Dominica continued the lessons, her pronunciation was somewhat unreliable. When she spoke, her English sounded a lot like Japanese and not very much like Sister Mary Josephine's version.

"The program—something—something—is Zero Hour." I wrote down what I thought some of the words were so I could look them up later. "Now a woman is talking. She says she's Orphan Ann—she sends greetings to Joe. She's asking him questions—Are you lonely? Do you know what your wife is doing? No one is at home—there are storms—big trouble." The reception became fuzzy, and I removed the headphones. "I couldn't understand most of what she said. It wasn't making too much sense. The woman kept talking to someone named Joe and telling him to go home."

"Strange, Joe is the name Americans use for their soldiers," said Uncle Hiroshi, "and that wasn't an American broadcast."

"But Orphan Ann sounded the same as Sister Mary Josephine, she must be an American."

"Hmm…if the program was meant for the Americans, it must be propaganda. That's something new."

"Why?" I asked.

"We were told that Japan would observe *bushido* and not use misleading information to undermine the enemy."

"Why?" Harumi asked.

"*Bushido* is the old code of the samurai. The Japanese warrior is supposed to treat the enemy with honor—not lies." Uncle Hiroshi clicked his tongue against his teeth in disapproval.

Not long afterward, we went to bed. Radio reception had become poor; besides, we were tired from working in the fields all day. In bed, as I snuggled under my *kakebuton*, I couldn't help but think about what I heard on the radio. Even though the outcome of the battles weren't told to us, it was clear Japan wasn't winning. While the Army and Navy were expected to follow rules of honor, lying messages contradicted those rules. What else didn't we know? Fortunately, my tiredness overtook my troubled thoughts, and I drifted off to sleep.

The next morning, as we were preparing to leave the house for the fields behind the drying barn, two people turned in from the road and made their way up our driveway. One was dressed in uniform and the other was Gorou. Their approach was slow; Gorou limped much more severely than usual. I was afraid that he had hurt himself, or someone had injured him.

"Who's that with Gorou?" Aunty Maiko asked.

"I don't know," Mama said.

"Why is Gorou walking like that?" Harumi asked. "Is he hurt?"

"I don't know what's wrong with Gorou, but he has a *Rikugun Jun-i* with him." Uncle Hiroshi pulled himself up to his full height and waited for Gorou and the soldier. "I doubt the warrant officer brings good news."

Chapter 9

Uncle Hiroshi stepped down from the porch and walked up to meet the officer. The two men acknowledged each other with slight bows of their heads.

"You are Hiroshi Kuroda?"

Uncle Hiroshi nodded.

The soldier pulled an envelope from inside his uniform jacket. "I have been sent to inform you about an official duty." The soldier turned away and gestured for Uncle Hiroshi to follow him. They walked down the driveway and continued talking, out of earshot.

"What do you think he wants?" Harumi asked. "We don't have any more animals for the army—unless they want our skinny little chickens." She walked around the side of the house, headed for the barn.

Mama and Aunty Maiko looked at each other and, without saying anything, turned and went into the house. Gorou and I stood on the porch; I motioned for him to sit down on the top step; and when he did, I joined him.

"Is something wrong?" I asked him. "You're limping a lot more than usual. Have you injured yourself?"

"Oh, yes, I'm in terrible agony." Gorou smiled in contradiction to his words. "It's the same lameness I always suffer whenever I'm around the army. I have found that the more unfit I am, the healthier I become."

"Like Uncle Hiroshi's 'old man' when he was on Okinawa." I laughed, partly at Gorou's ruse, but also with relief that he wasn't hurt. "Did the officer make you walk out here with him?"

"No, I was already on my way when he caught up with me." Gorou took an envelope from his pocket and handed it to me. "This came to the post office for you. Mrs. Higa asked me to deliver it."

"It's from Sayuri!" I looked at the familiar handwriting on the envelope. "I haven't heard from her since she left." I held the envelope in my hand and caressed it, as though I could absorb it through my skin.

"Open it," Gorou said. "Then you can tell me what she says."

"I don't want to be rude…," I hesitated.

"Go ahead."

I didn't wait for him to say more. I lifted the flap and, as carefully as I could, slid out a single sheet covered with small cramped writing.

14 June 1944

Dear Atsuko,

This is the first chance I've had to write. I don't know if this will reach you.

Mail delivery is unreliable and I heard the ferries hardly run anymore. We are living with my grandmother now. It isn't the best situation—there's a lot of friction between my mother and Papa's mother. But it's better than the situation of others. Many people have no homes. Huge groups constantly roam the streets and stay wherever they can find a place to settle. When we first started living on Okinawa, my father had work as a mechanic. But no more. There isn't any fuel. The streets are full of deserted automobiles and tractors are left standing in the fields. Many of the farms have been abandoned. That makes the food shortage worse. We have to stand in line nearly all day to be given an allotment of rice. It's never more than one cup each, most of the time not even that, and the quality is very poor. Sometimes it's more dirt and pebbles than grains of rice. Water is in short supply; we don't have enough to drink and can't do any cleaning. Enough of my complaints. I'm sure you have hardships as well. I wear your pearl always. I keep it under my blouse, out of sight and where I can feel it. It is a constant reminder of you, my friend, and the life we had before all this misery. I shelter it from the eyes of others—theft is a big problem here.

People are so desperate. Two good things, we have a place to stay, and so far, we are healthy. Many others have died of the hardships. I keep remembering how we worked in the peanut field. It won't be long and you will be harvesting them. I wish you could send me some. They would be treasured. Maybe the war will end soon and we can be together, eating peanuts on your farm and telling jokes like we used to.

Your always friend,
Sayuri

After I finished the letter, I sat, silently stared down at the words she had written, and thought about the privations Sayuri now faced. Her words, "misery," "hardships," and "desperate," were far removed from my friend who saw humor in practically every situation and kept me laughing with her silly jokes. *Would we ever be so carefree again?*

"How is she?" Gorou asked. "What has happened to their family?"

"Here." I handed the letter to him and waited for him to read it.

"Yes." Gorou sighed and gave the letter back. "I've seen this on Okinawa. People remove the tires from stranded automobiles and use the rubber to make shoes. It's impossible to buy anything, and everyone scrambles, looking for what they need."

"Worse than it is here on Iejima?" I folded the letter and slid it back in the envelope so I could keep it safe.

"Much worse—there are so many more people."

"What about the black market?"

"That's not always a good idea." Gorou hesitated. "The men in the black market often cheat people. I heard of one woman who bought a cartload of charcoal from the black market and was told to let the *rentan* dry. When they did, the briquettes crumbled because they were made of black mud. Then there is the danger of being caught by the *Keizai Keisatsu*."

"What are Economic Police?" I asked. "I've never heard of them."

"They confiscate illegal goods and arrest the offenders—both the sellers and the buyers."

"Do you think that's what the officer wants with Uncle Hiroshi?" My stomach did flip-flops at the thought. "That's how he bought our seeds."

"No. Look at them—they are just talking. If he came to arrest your uncle, he'd do more than talk. Besides, it has been over three months since your uncle used the black market. Hundreds of people have used it since then."

"I hope you are right. It would be horrible if Uncle Hiroshi were arrested."

"Try not to worry." Gorou stood up and smiled down at me. "I better leave now. I want to fish today, and I don't want the officer expecting me to accompany him back to town."

"Won't he catch up with you on the road?"

"I'm not headed that way. I'm going to Iwa Cove. I still have my boat hidden there."

"Be careful." I held out my hand to him.

"I will." Gorou took my hand in his larger one and gave a slight squeeze. "Remember, I told you I've been taking care of myself for a long time now. If I'm successful, I'll bring some fish back for your family."

"That would be much appreciated, and thank you for the letter."

"I was happy to bring it to you." He stepped down from the porch. "I'll leave a different way—behind the barn and across the fields. The shortcut allows me to avoid the officer. I'm going to exaggerate my limp, but don't be concerned—it's for show. Good-bye for now." Gorou limped slowly toward the drying barn, and before he disappeared around the corner, he turned and gave a final wave.

I looked down at my hands. In one I held the letter from Sayuri, and the other—the one that Gorou had held—still felt warm from his touch. My feelings were mixed up. While glad to receive word from my friend, her difficult life saddened me. As for Gorou, I didn't know what I felt. He acted caring toward me, but then he treated many people that way. He did say that if he brought fish back, it would be for the family, not just me. However, he didn't smile at the others and definitely didn't hold their hands. I imagined him behaving that way toward Mama and almost laughed out loud at the picture in my mind. Shaking my head at my silly ideas, I stood up and walked into the house.

Mama and Aunty Maiko were kneeling at the table, drinking tea, and speculating on what business the army had with Uncle Hiroshi. They looked up as I entered the room.

"What did you hear?" Mama asked. "Do you know what the officer wants of Hiroshi?"

"No, I only heard as much as you did—he's here about an official duty." I knelt next to Mama and held out my letter. "Gorou brought me this—a letter from Sayuri."

Mama read the letter aloud. A worry frown wrinkled her forehead.

"*Yare,*" Aunty Maiko said, her voice soft. "The circumstances on Okinawa seem much worse than here. All those poor people."

"Yes, it is all so troublesome." Mama handed the letter back to me.

"I'll be right back." I went to my bedroom, opened the chest, and placed Sayuri's letter on top of other notes I had from her. When I returned to the dining room, Uncle Hiroshi had come inside and joined the women at the table. The officer was not with him.

"What did he want?" Mama asked. "What official duty do you have?"

"Where is Harumi?" Uncle Hiroshi asked. "Everyone needs to hear. The duty involves all of us."

"She's in the barn," I said. "I'll go and bring her back." I found Harumi right where I thought she'd be. She sat in Mr. Brave's old stall, her back against the rough wooden boards and her knees drawn up. She had wrapped his harness around her hands, and she had been crying.

"What do you think has happened to Mr. Brave?" Harumi asked. "I can't help worrying about him. So many soldiers are dying, it must be the same for the horses."

"Mr. Brave is clever." I wanted to reassure my sister. "Remember how he escaped his pen and we weren't able to figure out how until we saw him nudge the latch loose? Besides, we don't know where he was sent. Maybe he's not anywhere near the fighting. He's such a fine horse, I wouldn't be surprised if the emperor kept Mr. Brave to pull his carriage."

"The same emperor who cares for all his people and looks after them?" Harumi sniffed her disbelief at what she said. "We were told in school that Japan is at war for the honor of the country and how much better it will be when we control Asia, instead of the Western devils. Hah!"

"I think we all have our doubts about that."

"What good will be accomplished if Japan rules all of Asia and we are all dead?"

"I don't know, but right now we can't stay in the barn. Uncle Hiroshi wants us to hear what the officer told him. He said we are part of the duty. Come on, let's go." I took the harness from Harumi and hung it on a peg, then helped brush the straw off her clothes before we left the barn.

The three adults were still at the table when Harumi and I rushed into the dining room. Mama had paper and a pencil while Uncle Hiroshi had two sheets of paper headed with the emperor's seal and filled with writing.

"This is the announcement for a change in policy for our community." Uncle Hiroshi held the papers in front of him and began to read:

> *The people of Iejima are to distribute/receive*
> *their food and supplies in a fair and honest system,*
> *regulated and managed by their neighborhood asso-*

ciation. The association will be responsible for determining the quantities to be provided by each farm and how they shall be allocated. Crop yields shall be estimated and quotas set prior to harvest. A predetermined percentage of all crops shall be forfeited to the military representatives of the Japanese Imperial Army now supervising Iejima. Another predetermined percentage will be given to the neighborhood association for distribution. Each farmer may keep the remainder of their crops after their quota has been met.

The neighborhood association shall be comprised of local residents and military personnel stationed on Iejima. The military commander of Iejima will review the work of the association. Any disputes or disparities will be adjudicated by said commander.

Uncle Hiroshi stopped reading and looked at us. "The announcement goes on to list the members of the neighborhood association. I am on that list."

"What does that mean?" Harumi asked.

"I will be part of the group that determines how much each farmer can keep, how much is turned over to the neighborhood association, and how much will be forfeited to the army."

"How do you decide the amounts?" I asked.

"Unfortunately, we don't have much choice. The percentages are already set, and they have been calculated on how much each farm should harvest based on its size."

"The numbers are not reasonable." Mama frowned as she looked at the columns of numbers on the second piece of paper. "They assume that the farms will all produce large crops—larger than usual. The percentage of food we give away will be based on an imaginary amount, not what is really there."

"But if we can keep a percentage, we should have enough," Harumi said.

"It doesn't work that way," Uncle Hiroshi said. "The government takes their percentage first, then the neighborhood association, and what remains is for us. If we have a bad season, the government could take everything."

"That's not right!" Harumi raised her hand as though she was going to thump the table; however, one glance from Mama stopped her in midair. "The people in charge don't need more of our food. That soldier who was here today already has a big round belly."

Mama stood up and walked over to the alcove that was our household shrine. She gazed at the scroll hanging over the small altar and touched the stone that had been placed there the day of Papa's funeral. Her lips moved silently as she asked for guidance from those who were no longer living. Then, just as I'd seen her do many times before, she pulled herself to her full height, squared her shoulders, and turned around to speak to us.

"It is difficult for a mother to consider depriving her children of food. But what choice do we have? We could attempt to deceive the government, but we won't. The Oshiro family has always been *shojiki*, and a family without its integrity has nothing of value. Hiroshi, what should we do in preparation for this new policy?"

"We need to declare how large our fields are and list what crops have been planted. We can start now."

Mama picked up the pencil and began writing. "We can list the fields, but they are split up, so we'll have to measure each one. The larger fields can be measured in *cho*, the smaller areas in *tan*." She recited the crop names as she wrote. "Peanuts…tobacco…melon… *daikon*…carrots…"

"This will be an important challenge for us." Aunty Maiko spoke for the first time.

"What do you mean?" I asked.

"We will need to work even harder to ensure our harvest is bountiful," she said. "How else can we have enough?"

"That's right," Harumi said. "I don't want to work all summer and end up with no food."

"Let's think about what we can do," Mama said. "We have seeds left, and it's still early summer. We can plant more rows."

"We need to make sure the plants receive enough water," I said. The thought that we could increase the yield of our crops began to improve the atmosphere in the room; the optimism was almost tangible. "Fortunately, our well is deep, and we have plenty of water."

"We can add fertilizer," Uncle Hiroshi said. "Plenty of manure from Mr. Brave is ready to be used. When they came for our animals, the soldiers didn't think to confiscate their manure."

"Why would the military want stinky, old fertilizer?" Harumi wrinkled her nose.

"Because they use it to make their stinky, old bombs," Uncle Hiroshi said, smiling.

"It's still morning," Mama brought the conversation back to making plans. "Now that we thought of a way to overcome this new obstacle, let's start working on it. I'll inspect the fields and determine where we can plant more seeds."

"I'll go with you," Aunty Maiko stood. "I'm still learning how to be a farmer, but I'll do whatever you tell me."

"I can fill the pushcart with manure and start adding it to the soil," Uncle Hiroshi said.

"Harumi and I will help you."

We left the house. Mama and Aunty Maiko walked down to the peanut field while the rest of us headed to the large pile of manure heaped behind the barn.

Chapter 10

We worked very hard for the rest of the summer. Before we could do more planting, we needed to prepare the soil—loosening it and adding fertilizer.

"This stinks." Harumi wrinkled her nose at the smell of the manure.

"I agree," I said. "But look at it this way—it's from Mr. Brave. Even though he isn't here anymore, he's still helping us."

"Yes, but this isn't the part of him I miss."

"Look at poor Uncle Hiroshi—he has it worse than we do. He has to load the manure in the cart and push it down from behind the barn."

"But it all seems so unfair. We're working more than ever, and we have to give most of our crops away."

"Think of the people who don't have any food, and no way of buying any. Think about what Sayuri wrote in her letter. People are starving. We would not be very honorable if we didn't share. Besides, grumbling makes it worse."

Harumi looked at me as though she was going say something; instead, she just sighed and, with a shrug, moved down the row. When I glanced at her later, I saw her taking out her frustrations by attacking the clumped dirt. Poor Harumi, life wasn't much fun for her that summer.

No extra tobacco was planted; we already had enough growing. Besides, even though we were obligated to produce a certain amount, it wouldn't do much good to grow any more of it. We always sold the entire crop to the Japanese Tobacco Company. Instead, we planted extra rows of vegetables, hoping to double the yield. Because we planted the second set of rows two months after the first, we'd harvest in two stages. That would make it easier for us. Fortunately, our island was far enough south so that we had a long growing season. But while everything was growing, we were busy.

The summer of 1944 was very dry, and we needed to provide a constant supply of water to the fields. Mama worried that our wells would go dry. In July, it usually rained frequently, but not that summer, and the well by the tobacco field began pumping dirty water. We started work very early in the morning and watered before the day's heat could evaporate our efforts. Every plant that thrived was precious, and we mourned, when despite our diligence, some shriveled and died.

During that summer, Uncle Hiroshi worked with the neighborhood association. They went from farm to farm to check the crops. He reported that everyone suffered from the dry conditions and their harvests would probably be smaller than usual.

"The farmers are trying their best, but the crops are not going to be abundant," Uncle Hiroshi said after one of his inspection tours in the middle of July. "The people of Iejima will more than likely experience shortages again."

That evening we sat in Uncle Hiroshi and Aunty Maiko's room after dinner and listened to the radio. We hardly spent our time like this anymore. After working long, hard hours in the fields, we usually had a late meal, cleaned up, and went to bed early. That night was different. Gorou had come to our farm that afternoon. Not only did he bring a fish for us, but he also stayed and worked with us for the rest of the day. With his help, we were able to accomplish more than usual.

Mama and Aunty Maiko made an excellent dinner that evening, and as we gathered around the table, it was almost festive—with Gorou as a guest and more food than we normally had. But later, listening to the broadcasts from Tokyo, the conversation turned to the war. We discovered there were two versions of events—the "official" one from the government and what really was happening.

"The military announces the fighting in the Philippine Sea turned out exactly as expected," Uncle Hiroshi reported. "They say they are ready for the next encounter."

"That means the government is happy Japan lost." Gorou's voice reflected his disgust.

"What do you mean?" Aunty Maiko asked.

"We lost that battle," Gorou said. "We lost troops, ships, and airplanes. The Japanese Imperial Navy has been greatly damaged."

"How can we ready for fighting then?" I asked.

"The Navy plans to use the useless aircraft carriers for decoys— to lure the Americans into a trap. It's all the ships are good for now," Gorou said.

"How do you know all this?" Harumi asked.

"I know some of the officers." When Gorou saw our puzzled looks, he continued, "I have a connection with a supply sergeant. I don't entirely trust him, but we do business."

"What business is that?" Aunty Maiko's voice was soft.

"I trade fish for fuel to use on my boat."

"How valuable is a fish that you can get enough fuel?" Harumi asked.

"Black market," I whispered in her ear.

"Oh." Her mouth formed a small circle.

"Does this sergeant know so much that he can tell you information?" Uncle Hiroshi asked.

"No," Gorou said. "My twisted foot makes some people think that my mind is also deformed. They treat me as though I have no understanding at all, and the officers talk freely in front of me."

"Of course you don't give them any reason to think otherwise." I remembered how Gorou had explained to me how bad his limp became in front of the military.

"I discovered that if I slouch to favor my bad foot and have an empty expression, I'm in a position to do some valuable listening."

"What have you heard lately?" Uncle Hiroshi asked.

"The Americans have started bombing Tokyo. And the Navy is worried about losing the Marianas."

"Would losing the Marianas be terrible?" Mama asked. "Are they important to Japan?"

"They are not important themselves," Uncle Hiroshi explained. "But if we lose control of the islands, then we lose control of the shipping lanes." He then turned back to Gorou. "Have you heard any talk of Prime Minister Tojo?"

"He has become very unpopular. The other day I heard Captain Yamada say Tojo will soon be forced to resign."

"Is that good?" Harumi asked. "Does it mean that the war will end?"

"It could be good," Uncle Hiroshi said. "But it could also mean more chaos. Tojo was in charge of most of Japan."

The Zero Hour program began on the radio, and no one wanted to listen to the propaganda broadcast. It was hard to understand, and what I could translate from English was confusing. We finished straightening up and prepared for bed. Gorou was spending the night in the small building where he stayed before. We wouldn't see him in the morning; he planned to leave before dawn.

I lay on my futon and thought about our conversation. It was frightening to think about the Americans bombing Tokyo. All those people—dead. And most of them innocent victims. I didn't feel too sorry for all the Japanese generals who made the decisions that led up to this, but my heart ached for all the families that had been destroyed and everyone who suffered. If Tojo was forced from his position, he probably deserved it. Then I began to worry about plans for the "decoy ships." What if they were going to be used to lure the Americans into battle near us? Okinawa was a major location. Could it be a target?

With all those troubling thoughts, it took me a long time to fall asleep that night.

*****

Because of the drought, our first harvest in August wasn't as large as we wanted. By the end of July, the well in the fields had gone dry, and we now depended solely on the well by the kitchen for all water—cooking, cleaning, drinking, and watering. Luckily it rained in August, and that restored some of our supply, giving us hope for a better second harvest.

The men in the neighborhood association measured, weighed, and divided the yield. We weren't surprised to learn the portion we could keep was very small. However, with the second harvest in October, we would be able to keep most of it. A disturbing thought poked at my brain, suggesting it was probably not wise to put too much faith in what we were told about the second harvest—the military had given us so many reasons to distrust them.

On the day the men arrived to take the portions designated for the army and the neighborhood association, a large truck came to the farm. That was a surprise, since there was such a fuel shortage. However, the army somehow managed to find enough gas for the truck to transport their food.

In the days after the first harvest, we pickled and canned the vegetables we were allowed to keep. By the time we finished, it was time to dig the peanuts. All this was new for Aunty Maiko, and her excitement at pulling peanuts from the earth was infectious.

"How do you know when they're ready?" Aunty Maiko walked with us across the road to the peanut field. I had a pitchfork, Harumi carried a shovel, and Aunty carried a trowel along with the lunch basket.

"Before the plants are ready, they start to lose their green color and the leaves turn yellow. That's because the kernels need the plant's food," I said. "The leaves began to change last week. Now we'll inspect some pods."

We reached the fields, and I pulled up a few random pods. "See—these are ready. The veins inside the pods are dark." I removed a kernel and held it out to Aunty Maiko. "Look at the paper." I slid the covering off the peanut. "The paper is light pink and feels papery. The soil feels good also—not too wet, not too dry. We can dig up the plants."

Harumi and I showed Aunty Maiko how to dig up the whole plant and gently shake off the loose dirt clinging to the roots. We laid the plants along the edges of the rows. Uncle Hiroshi brought the pushcart to the field and carefully loaded it.

"Our timing is good. If we wait too long, the pods break off in the soil and are hard to find." I was happy with the amount of peanuts we gathered. All of our hard work paid off—we not only had many plants, they also had abundant pods clinging to them.

"What do we do next?" Aunty Maiko asked. "Do we roast them?"

"Not yet," Harumi said. "Uncle Hiroshi will take them to the drying barn."

"That's right," I said. "They're placed with the peanuts facing upward for two weeks so they dry out."

"How do you know when they're ready?" Aunty Maiko asked.

"The leaves turn dry and crumbly," I said. "That's when we pull the nuts off the plants."

"Then it's time to cut and dry the tobacco," Harumi said.

"The work on a farm never ends, does it?" Aunty Maiko asked.

"No, it doesn't, and this year, there will be even more, we have our second harvest in October," I said.

"*Yare*, we have so much to do." Aunty Maiko looked around at all the plants we had dug. "I think it's time for us to eat lunch."

We sat in the shade and ate. After finishing our meal and while we rested on the ground, we received two visitors. One was Uncle Hiroshi, who brought the cart down for a second time to load up plants to take to Mama in the drying barn. The second person, Gorou, walked up the gulch from Iwa Cove and joined us.

"I have more war news," he said. "The Americans have taken Guam."

"What does that mean? For us?" Aunty Maiko asked.

"The Americans now control all the oil supplies for Japan," Gorou said. "It won't be fuel shortages anymore, there won't be any fuel at all. The Japanese Navy will not be able to run their ships."

"I wonder what will happen now," I said.

"I know." Harumi kicked her shovel. "Nothing good. We're all going to die."

Chapter 11

Aunty Maiko reached over and touched Harumi on the arm. "Surely our situation isn't entirely hopeless. We still have each other and the farm."

While I sympathized with Harumi's distress, I was glad that Aunty Maiko was there to calm her down after her outburst.

"Don't you think *shimen soka**?" Harumi's voice was quieter.

"No, we're not desperate," Aunty Maiko said. "Look how hard we've worked, and how much we've accomplished. Harvest will be larger than originally planned. We will have enough food for ourselves, as well as some to share with others. Think how fortunate that is."

Aunty Maiko continued speaking to Harumi in a soft voice while Gorou turned to me and said, "I'm sorry for bringing more bad news."

"It's not your fault Japan has lost again." I picked up a shovel and began digging. "Unfortunately, defeat is accompanied by so many other hardships." I lifted a plant from the dirt, loosened the dirt from the peanuts, and laid it down on the ground.

"Let me help." Gorou picked up Harumi's shovel and dug the row across from me.

"We've been at war for so long, it's practically all I've ever known, and it's been worse for Harumi."

"Why do you think it's harder for your sister?"

"Because when I was her age, our soldiers were victorious. We were taught pride in their exploits. It was easy to believe that Japan would control Asia and achieve peace and prosperity. Harumi doesn't

---

* Japanese idiom—Defeat is clear; situation is desperate beyond hope

94

have those memories. First, she was only ten when Papa died, and our life became more difficult. Then she had to go to school away from home, and she was faced with an unpleasant situation—a harsh teacher and endless war drills. Now we've lost so much—Mr. Brave, part of our crops, and so many soldiers have been killed."

We finished the two rows and moved on to the next set, working side by side. The August afternoon's temperature rose, and I had to pause several times to wipe the sweat from my face.

"Atsuko, you don't spend much energy thinking about yourself, do you?" Gorou asked.

"What do you mean?"

"You are always concerned about others. I've seen you worry about your Uncle Hiroshi, your mother, Harumi, and your friend Sayuri, but never yourself."

"But I'm fine."

"Yes, you are."

I looked up and saw Gorou staring at me intently. Confused, I quickly looked back down and bent over to pull a peanut plant up. "We have to be careful how we remove the dirt from the peanuts." I spoke to cover up my awkwardness.

"If you ever need help, I hope you will ask me."

"But, Gorou, you already help us so much. We shouldn't take advantage."

"Your uncle, along with many others, has been generous to me, I can never repay all the kindness I have received. But that's not exactly what I meant."

Before our conversation could go any further, Uncle Hiroshi came down the row to pick up the plants and take them back to the drying barn. By the time he left, Harumi and Aunty Maiko joined us, the moment had passed, and our conversation became general.

"How's your friend Miss Singer?" Gorou asked Harumi. "Is she still noisy?"

"She's not noisy!" Harumi stuck her tongue out. "Miss Singer has a beautiful voice, but she doesn't use it as much anymore."

"Oh?"

"She's bigger now and has discovered hunting. If she wants to capture mice, she has to be quiet. Of course, when she catches one and brings it inside, she always announces her success."

"Even if she delivers it to me—in the middle of the night—in my bed." Harumi laughed when I said this, and I thought how Harumi's mood had changed so quickly from her despair of a few minutes before. I was always surprised by how swiftly she could go from one emotion to the opposite.

"Miss Singer will earn her keep, now we have the peanuts to save from mice and rats," Harumi said.

"Can she catch all of them?" Gorou looked skeptical.

"No, but we've made it difficult for them to reach the peanuts while they are drying," I said. "We wrapped tin strips around the legs of the drying tables. Rats and mice have a hard time climbing metal, and with Miss Singer on patrol, not too many rodents loiter in the barn."

With Gorou's help, we finished harvesting the peanuts by the end of the day. Uncle Hiroshi took the plants along with their bounty up to the barn where he and Mama set them upside down on the tables. It was a good crop. After contributing the amount required, we would still have a considerable quantity left for ourselves.

Gorou left when the last of the peanut plants had been dug. Aunty Maiko invited him to stay for our evening meal, but he said he needed to check on his boat and meet someone in town.

"We were lucky to have such good help today," Aunty Maiko said. We knelt around the table eating the stew Mama prepared earlier. "What will we do next with the peanuts?"

"We don't have to do anything for a while," Harumi said. "They have to dry."

"When the leaves crumble, then we move them to the cellar—to stay cool until we roast them," I said.

"That's the best part," Harumi said. "They smell wonderful while they're roasting."

"When Papa was still alive, he took me to Okinawa, and we sold peanuts to the soldiers."

I told Aunty Maiko and Uncle Hiroshi about how my father and I made money from the peanuts. Standing outside the gates of the army base, Papa and I would prepare the nuts on a brazier heated with charcoal. They smelled so tantalizing, roasting in the autumn air; we sold small bags of peanuts as fast as they were ready.

"Hiroshi, does that remind you of anything?" Aunty Maiko asked. "When we were in London?"

Uncle Hiroshi nodded. "Why don't you tell the girls?"

"It was winter when we were in London," Aunty Maiko began. "It was very cold. England is much colder than here. We were outside the entrance to the British Museum, and a man stood in front of the main entrance with his brazier."

"Was he selling peanuts?" Harumi asked. "Do they grow them in England?"

"No, he wasn't selling peanuts," Aunty Maiko said. "He was selling chestnuts."

"Like *kurigohan*?" I asked.

"No, they weren't with rice," Uncle Hiroshi said. "Just the roasted chestnuts."

"Were they the same as ours?" Mama asked.

"No, they are not as sweet," Aunty Maiko said. "What I liked best about seeing chestnuts sold on the street from a brazier was realizing we were halfway around the world and some things were the same."

"And now we are at war with the West." Uncle Hiroshi shook his head. "If we saw a Westerner, he would shoot us, or we would kill him."

"We don't need to worry about seeing the enemy." Mama hit the table with the flat of her hand. "Our next concern is the tobacco. I inspected the plants today, and they are beginning to turn yellow."

"Do we start to cut tomorrow?" Harumi asked.

"We will cut tomorrow—but you won't," Mama said. "I don't want you handling a tobacco knife yet."

"Why not?" Harumi asked. "I'm just as strong as an adult. This is unfair."

"You'll be more valuable if you still have both your feet and arms." Mama's tone let Harumi know that she was done discussing the matter, and Harumi wisely quit protesting.

"Do you want Harumi and me to 'stick' the tobacco?" I asked. That was the job we had last year. Tobacco sticks had a spear on one end. After the tobacco stalk had been cut down, we would pierce it with the spear and thread it on the stick that had been driven into the ground. Each stick held as many stalks as we could fit on it. As long as it didn't rain, we could leave the sticks outside; however, when we moved the peanuts to the cellar, we usually moved the tobacco into the drying barn. In the past, trucks from the tobacco company came and took the tobacco when it was done curing. With the shortage of fuel, I didn't know if they would come anymore. *What would we do without the money from our tobacco crop?*

"Hiroshi and I will cut the stalks. Maiko, Harumi, and you can 'stick' them," Mama said. "It should go quickly, with such good help."

After spending all day digging up peanuts and knowing tomorrow would be just as much work, we all went to bed shortly after the sun went down. I was glad to be alone with my thoughts. I replayed my conversation with Gorou. This was the second time he said something to me that could be considered personal. But what did he mean by "not exactly what I meant"? What was his intent? Was it significant when he held my hand that day on the porch? I touched the carved elephant that Sayuri gave me the last time I saw her. It hung around my neck as a constant reminder of our friendship, and rubbing it had become a comforting habit. If elephants possessed the wisdom they were said to have, I could certainly benefit from some insight given to me by the jade figurine I wore. No such intelligence came to mind, and I was very tired—too tired to stay awake and think.

*****

We were lucky. It didn't rain for the rest of August, and we could leave the tobacco outside to dry. When it was finished curing, the Japanese Tobacco Company found enough fuel for a truck to take our crop. They didn't pay as much as usual, but at least we received some money to help us through the winter.

In September we had a short respite from the intense work we had endured. The first harvest was done; and the second, smaller one wouldn't be ready for a few weeks. Autumn was my favorite season. Under ordinary circumstances, our hardest work of the year was finished, fall colors brightened our lives, and on September sixteenth, I celebrated my eighteenth birthday. On that day, Mama told me she thought of me as an adult and I should consider myself one as well. "You've been doing the work of a grown-up," Mama said. "I want you to know how much I appreciate what you do on the farm and how much I rely on you. Someday, when the war is over, I hope that you can do something for yourself—follow your heart's desire, maybe go to university."

"Thanks, Mama," I said. Her remarks surprised me. Mama didn't talk so openly very often; she usually kept her feelings to herself.

The rest of the day brought more surprises. Harumi, with help from Mama, was going to make my birthday dinner—one of the few remaining chickens was to be sacrificed. Aunty Maiko gave me a beautiful silk jacket that she had sewn and embroidered. It was the most wonderful item of clothing I had ever owned.

"This is from your Uncle Hiroshi and me," Aunty Maiko said. "He provided all the material, and I sewed it."

"When did you make it?" I asked. "I never saw you working on it."

"I stole a minute here and there, it was nothing."

"I think you stole more than minutes." I held the jacket close. "It's beautiful! Thank you!"

Later that afternoon, I sat on the porch, wore my new jacket, and indulged myself by reading from my book of poetry. From a small collection of haiku by Matsuo Basho, I found one that reminded me of September—the month of my favorite flower.

> *Drinking morning tea,*
> *The monk is peaceful.*
> *The chrysanthemum blooms.*

Not long before dinnertime, I saw someone walking up our driveway. It was Gorou. At first I thought he had news for us or wanted to talk with Uncle Hiroshi. I was wrong on both counts.

Harumi must have been watching from inside. She rushed out to the porch. "You came!" She turned to me. "It's another surprise for your birthday—we invited Gorou. Are you surprised? Are you glad?"

"That's very nice," I said. I looked at Gorou. "We are having a special dinner—it's a good evening to be here." Once again, I felt awkward and didn't know what to say. It was a little embarrassing to have my family invite a man for my birthday dinner—even if it was someone as familiar as Gorou.

Gorou came up the porch stairs and held out a bouquet. "I remembered that your favorite flower is the chrysanthemum." He smiled at me. "I found these down by the lake. It's not much, but I hope you like them."

"They are beautiful. I do like chrysanthemums. Thank you. I'll take them inside and put them in a vase. Such pretty flowers will make the dining room look festive."

We entered the house; Aunty Maiko was setting the table, and Mama came out from the kitchen. "Gorou, I'm glad you could make it for Atsuko's birthday. Harumi, go find Hiroshi, tell him it's time to eat. Atsuko, Gorou, wait here. Maiko and I will bring in the food."

When I knelt down with my family and Gorou that day, it was such a pleasant occasion, all the hardships we had been suffering faded away for a short time. No matter what the future brought, I was a fortunate person.

Chapter 12

The second harvest in October followed the brief break we enjoyed in September. When the crops were ready to be gathered, we were busier than ever. Though we were obligated to contribute most of our yield in August, almost everything reaped in October we kept and preserved for the winter ahead.

Mama organized a system. Uncle Hiroshi and Harumi gathered the crops and brought them to an outbuilding behind the kitchen. Laid on a long table, I inspected the plants and cleaned them. *Daikons* remained on a shelf because the radishes needed to dry out before being pickled. I put the other vegetables in bushel baskets and took them into the kitchen where Mama and Aunty Maiko finished the process of preserving them.

In the past, Mama used several different methods of pickling. She soaked vegetables in salt, sugar, vinegar, soy sauce, sake, malted rice, or hot mustard. Sometimes she used a combination of ingredients. A pickled vegetable could have a variety of tastes, depending on what ingredient fermented it. However, this year she mostly used salt. It was impossible for her to get anything else. The only exception was her plan to make *kasuzuke*. She had *sake* to use on some of the white melons. I was glad; the melons pickled this way were sweet and mild, a favorite of mine.

Our family owned an extensive collection of *tsukemonoki*, and the glass pickle presses had been cleaned and lined up in the kitchen waiting for Mama and Aunty Maiko. The baskets of cucumbers, carrots, cabbage, turnips, and onions became empty; they filled the large jars. On an afternoon toward the end of October, we were in the middle of picking, cleaning, and pickling cucumbers when an unexpected visitor interrupted us. A horse-drawn wagon I didn't immediately recognize came up the driveway. Thinking of all the unpleasantness we endured when visited by uninvited strangers, I was sure more trouble was coming to my family. As the wagon drew closer, I could see the driver. A wave of relief, and maybe anticipation, swept over me at the sight of Gorou handling the reins. I also identified the horse; it belonged to our neighbor, Mr. Nishiyama. *But a wagon? Why?* I hadn't seen Gorou since my birthday dinner and didn't know what he'd been doing for the past month. I supposed he had been fishing, but maybe I was wrong.

"Hello!" Uncle Hiroshi walked around the barn and went up to the wagon. "It looks like you were successful."

"Hero!" Harumi, who had followed Uncle Hiroshi, ran up to the horse and began stroking its neck and head. "Why do you have Mr. Nishiyama's horse and wagon?"

"He loaned them to me for a special errand." Gorou smiled down at Harumi then looked at Uncle Hiroshi. "Do you want to tell everyone? After all, it is your story."

"Hiroshi, what's this all about?" Aunty Maiko joined us in the driveway. Mama stood next to her, wiping her hands with a towel.

"Gorou here was able to work some wizardry." Uncle Hiroshi grinned. "He took some magic beans and turned them into treasure."

"What do you mean magic beans?" Mama asked.

"Well, money actually, but magic beans sound better." Uncle Hiroshi gestured to the back of the wagon. "Look at what we have."

I looked over the side of the wagon. Five large canvas bags were piled on the wagon's bed. 米 was printed on each bag in red ink. "You brought rice! Where? How? Is it all for us?"

"Yes, the rice is for our family." Uncle Hiroshi watched us staring at the sacks; he grinned even more. "After we harvested the tobacco, I realized we had more than we needed for the contract. Gorou and I came up with a plan for him to trade the surplus for food. We managed to keep it a secret. I hope it is a pleasant surprise."

"It's much better than pleasant. This is stupendous!" I couldn't believe our good fortune. We hadn't had this much rice since Papa was alive. After the hardships we suffered last year, our prospects for the coming winter looked promising.

"Hiroshi and I will unload the bags," Gorou said. "Harumi, would you like to hold the reins and guide Hero around to the back?"

Harumi looked up from where she stood next to the horse. "I would rather lead him with the harness and walk next to him—like I used to with Mr. Brave. Can I?"

"I don't see why not," Gorou said.

"Gorou, we'll be eating dinner in a few hours. Do you have time to stay?" Mama asked.

"I'd like to," he said. "Unfortunately, I need to return the horse and wagon to Nishiyama-san. I promised him I'd have them back before four o'clock."

"Why don't you come back?" Harumi asked. "We never get to see you anymore. Please?"

"Harumi's right, we'd like to have your company," Aunty Maiko said. "Do you have time?"

"I could return." Gorou looked at me when he spoke, a question in his eyes.

"Please do." I smiled at him.

"I will." Gorou returned the smile. "Let's take care of this rice, then I can leave and come back before it's too late."

"We look forward to spending the evening with you," Uncle Hiroshi said. "You always have war news for us. We've learned there's fighting in the Philippines, but we haven't been told very much about it. Do you know anything?"

"I've heard." A shadow passed over Gorou's face. "We can talk about it later. But now let's get this rice safely packed away."

While Uncle Hiroshi and Gorou moved the bags of rice to storage and Harumi fed an apple to Hero, the rest of us returned to cleaning and pickling the last of the cucumbers. When all the vegetables we prepared were soaking in brine, Aunty Maiko and I carried the jars down to the root cellar where we did the final step—placing lids weighted down with rocks on the jars. The pressure of the lids forced liquid from the vegetables and added to the flavors.

"*Yare*, we certainly accomplished a great deal today." Aunty Maiko stood back and looked at the rows of jars placed along the shelves. "I never realized how much was involved in pickling."

"The next step is the easiest—when they're ready, when they become stinky-good, we eat." I looked at Aunty Maiko; she appeared tired. "I hope you are not sorry that you've become a farmer. It's not always as hard as it's been this year."

"I have no regrets." Aunty Maiko brushed a strand of hair away from her face. "I must admit, the amount of work has been a surprise. But I wouldn't want to be anywhere else than here with Hiroshi and your family. We were fortunate to have a place to stay after we closed the store."

"It's not glamorous, like your life as a model seamstress and traveling the world."

"Oh, Atsuko, quite often, my life was not glamorous. Training was long and difficult. I spent many hours bent over a sewing machine, trying to please a demanding instructor. More than once I wanted to quit."

"Why didn't you?" I asked.

"Because I needed a job. Faced with a lot of unpleasant choices, it appeared to be the best one. I worked in a clean shop. I knew if I was successful, I could enjoy a decent life. And now I'm at a different stage of my life. Now Hiroshi and I benefit from having a family. Enough talk, I should go back to the kitchen and help your mother."

"Aunty Maiko, you're tired. I'll go help Mama—why don't you rest until dinner?"

"I say all three of us should make dinner. I'm sure that everyone is tired, and if we work together, it will go quicker."

We rejoined Mama in the now-clean kitchen and, under her direction, put together our evening meal. By the time the food was ready and Harumi had prepared the dining room, Gorou returned to join us. Considering how hard we worked that day, we put together an excellent meal. We had fresh tomatoes and a salad of cucumbers and onions marinated in rice vinegar with red pepper flakes. The best part of the meal was the *origiri*. The rice balls contained small bits of salmon and were wrapped with seaweed. With the second harvest almost finished and the arrival of the rice, our dinner became a celebration. It wasn't until we drank tea afterward that the conversation became more serious.

"Gorou, can I ask you a question?" Harumi looked across the table at him. "How come Mr. Nishiyama still has Hero when we had to give Mr. Brave to the army?"

"Probably because Hero is over twenty years old and moves very slowly. Mr. Brave was only eight years old and much healthier. If Hero were in the army, he'd need a lot of care."

"It still isn't fair," Harumi said. "Without Mr. Brave, we've had to work really hard."

"Harumi—" Mama frowned.

"I understand how you feel." Aunty Maiko reached and put her hand on Harumi's arm. "We all felt bad when Mr. Brave had to leave and you lost a good friend."

"Gorou, you said there was war news," Uncle Hiroshi said. "What has happened in the Philippines?"

"The Americans, along with the Australians, have come back. They are fighting in Leyte Gulf, and it is not going well for us."

"Is it as bad as the battle in August?" Uncle Hiroshi asked.

"Worse," Gorou said.

Just a few years before, our forces invaded the Philippines. We learned Japan helped the country and established a better government for them. I remembered the official message was to be proud of our empire for all the advantages the Filipinos would have after the Americans were driven out. Many Americans were captured on the Bataan Peninsula, and we were told what had happened to the soldiers afterward—a long, grueling march—would discourage them from ever trying to control the Japanese Empire. From what Gorou told us, that wasn't true.

"I heard the fight has been a huge naval battle," Uncle Hiroshi said.

"It is," Gorou said. "Unfortunately, many of our ships are useless. Some of them were damaged in August, and others don't have enough fuel to operate."

"Have you heard of any special plans?" I asked. "Radio broadcasts never tell us what is really happening. They just keep telling us to be proud of our empire for the noble efforts of our soldiers."

"There is a new fighting unit—they are called *kamikaze*," Gorou said.

"God wind?" Harumi looked puzzled. "Does that mean we have soldiers who will never die?"

"Just the opposite," Gorou said. "They are trained pilots who fly suicide missions."

"What are they expected to do?" Mama asked.

"The best Japanese pilots were asked to volunteer for the unit," Gorou said. "According to my friend, the supply officer, every one of them raised their hands."

"I know how the army works," Uncle Hiroshi said. "They would have been severely punished if they didn't."

"True, pilots are treated cruelly even under ordinary circumstances," Gorou said. "The men in this unit are equipped with aircraft that become weapons. Loaded with bombs, torpedoes, or full fuel tanks, the planes are flown into enemy ships, causing as much damage as possible."

"So the pilots know they are going to die—before they take off?" Harumi asked. "I wouldn't do it."

"You wouldn't have a choice," I said. "Luckily, no one is going to make you."

"Still, I wouldn't."

I didn't want to start a futile argument with my little sister and decided not to answer her back again.

"The military tradition of Japan includes a philosophy that sounds noble, but I've begun to doubt its wisdom." Uncle Hiroshi spoke slowly, as if he weighed each word. "I have come to disagree with the idea we should prefer death over defeat or shame. Every day we work hard to survive. We even help others. That seems more noble to me."

"You probably don't want to let anyone outside your house hear you talk like that," Gorou said. "Those are thoughts I keep to myself whenever I have dealings with the military."

"It is sad that in Japan, a country dedicated to loyalty and honor, we are forced to use deception." Mama shook her head.

"Atsuko, you might find this interesting," Gorou said. "I was told the pilots recite 'Yamato Spirit' before they go on their missions."

"That's a death poem," I said. "I know it." I recited it for the group:

> Asked about the soul of Japan,
> I would say
> That it is
> Like wild cherry blossoms
> Glowing in the morning sun.

"I don't get it," Harumi said. "How is that a death poem? No one dies. It's not even very sad."

"I think for the young pilots, it's sad," Aunty Maiko sad. "They are the wild cherry blossoms destroyed by the morning sun." Everyone became silent after she said that.

"We have had enough of all this war talk," Mama said after a few minutes. "We can find better things to talk about. Besides, it's getting late. Harumi, you and I will clean the dishes and put them away before you go to bed."

While Mama and Harumi went into the kitchen to wash dishes, Aunty Maiko and Uncle Hiroshi left for their room.

"Would you like another cup of tea?" I asked Gorou. I was very conscious of the fact that the two of us were left alone, and I felt a little awkward.

"No, thank you. I have to be going soon. I told Nishiyama-san I would take him fishing early tomorrow—to pay him back for letting me use his horse and wagon."

"I want to know something," I said. "How did you manage to trade tobacco for rice? I didn't think there was that much rice in all of Japan."

"In some places, rice is plentiful. But I don't think it would be a very good idea if I told you how I obtained it."

"The black market? That's dangerous. If you were caught—"

"It wasn't the black market, I swear. But that's all I'll tell you." Gorou stood up and held his hand out. "Come, walk me to the door."

"Gorou?" We had reached the door, and Gorou was putting on his outdoor shoes.

"Yes?" He looked up at me.

"Someday, when the war is over, will you tell me how you were able to trade for rice?"

Gorou laughed and stood up straight. "When the war is over, I'll tell you all my secrets."

He reached over and ran his finger softly down my face. "All my secrets." And then he was gone.

Chapter 13

October ended with crashing thunderstorms. They broke the oppressive heat and brought much-needed rain. Luckily for us, the downpours didn't strike until we finished gathering our crops. The storms faded away, leaving Iejima to slip gradually toward winter. That didn't mean the weather turned harsh. It did mean the uncomfortable heat no longer bore down on us, and we could enjoy the milder temperatures that came with November.

We still had neverending work on the farm, but the pressure to finish everything quickly faded. Once the crops were harvested, we cleared the fields, leaving them ready for the next planting season. It was fortunate our efforts became less urgent; the coming of winter meant the days grew shorter. Mama let us sleep later, and in the evenings, we spent time together—listening to the radio or talking—instead of stumbling off to bed, exhausted from long hours in the fields.

One afternoon in late November as I took advantage of the dry day to sweep the front porch, I heard the sound of a wagon. When I saw Nishiyama-san's horse, I momentarily thought that Gorou had come to our farm. I hadn't seen him since October when he brought the bags of rice. As much as I thought about what he said to me that day, I had more questions than answers. I understood he couldn't tell me how he acquired the rice—illegal purchases were dangerous—but I wondered what he meant by "all my secrets." What didn't I know about him? However, I wasn't going to discover any more right then; Mr. Nishiyama sat on the wagon's bench, holding the reins. He was alone.

I walked up to Hero and grabbed the harness next to his head while our elderly neighbor climbed down from his perch. Holding the horse steady was a good idea; Mr. Nishiyama moved slowly, his joints stiff with age. When he stood on the ground, he turned and bowed in my direction; I returned the gesture.

Uncle Hiroshi came around the side of the house and walked up to us. "It is an honor to have you visit." He bowed to Mr. Nishiyama and received one in return. "Come into our house. Join us for *cha*."

"You are kind. I would appreciate some tea." Mr. Nishiyama wrapped the reins around the railing and stepped up to the porch. "Hero is like me, old and tired. He will wait patiently here until it is time to return home." He bowed to Mama, who came out to the porch and greeted our guest.

Inside, we knelt around the table, and Aunty Maiko poured tea for us; and when she finished, I took the pot and poured hers. Mama placed a plate of spiced rice crackers on the table, and Uncle Hiroshi passed them around. It wasn't until after we ate and drank that Mr. Nishiyama told us the purpose of his visit.

"I was in town this morning, and Higa-san at the post office asked me to bring this letter to you." Mr. Nishiyama handed an envelope to Mama.

At first I thought it might be from Sayuri, but I was wrong.

"This is from Okinawa." Mama unfolded the thin piece of stationery and read the message written on it, frowning as she did so. "It's from Yumiko. She sent this letter in July. Oh dear, she writes that Mamoru has died. She will not be returning. Instead, she plans to stay with her daughter. They haven't received any news of her son-in-law. They are afraid that he is dead also."

My initial reaction to the news was sorrow. Mamoru, our farmhand, and Yumiko, his wife, had been part of my life for as long as I could remember. Now he was gone, and Yumiko wasn't coming back. While news of Mamoru's death saddened me, I wasn't surprised to learn Yumiko did not intend to return. When they left in the spring, I felt their departure was final. It was just one of the many losses we suffered because of the war.

Mama looked down at the letter, as though, if she stared at the writing long enough, the message would change. Then she sighed and carefully folded and slipped the letter back into the envelope. Holding it, she stood and walked over to the alcove that was our shrine. She slid the letter underneath a smooth, black stone.

"Poor Mamoru, he has been dead for over four months, and we just now find out. Poor Yumiko, I don't know how she will manage. I don't suppose..." Mama looked at Uncle Hiroshi.

"No, Arisu," Uncle Hiroshi said. "I don't see how we can do anything for her. Anything we send would certainly not reach her, and travel is so difficult now."

"You're right," Mama said, "but I feel that I should be able to do something. I will write back to Yumiko and express my sorrow. I wish we could share some of our food with her."

"Unfortunately, I agree with Hiroshi," Mr. Nishiyama said. "I have sent packages to my children on Okinawa that they have never received. You will have better luck with a letter—but it won't be delivered very quickly."

"May I give Hero a—?" Harumi, who had just walked into the room, started to ask a question but stopped when she saw our expressions. "What's wrong? Should I leave?"

"No, you can stay," Mama said. "Mr. Nishiyama has brought us a letter from Yumiko. Mamoru died—he died in July."

"Oh, this stupid war! I hate it!" Tears streamed down Harumi's face.

"It wasn't the war," Mama said. "Not directly. Mamoru was old—nearly ninety—and he worked hard all his life."

"But he left because of the war," Harumi said. "If he stayed with us, we could have taken care of him." She turned and walked to the kitchen. When Harumi came back, she had a carrot. "May I give this to Hero?" Mama nodded, and Harumi went outside where Hero stood, half asleep in the afternoon sun.

"I'm sorry I brought bad news." Mr. Nishiyama sighed. "Seems as though it's the only kind we receive these days. I keep checking with the post office, but I haven't had word from my son for over a year. Not hearing from him is agony, and yet, no news gives me a sliver of hope."

"Do you know where your son is fighting?" Aunty Maiko's voice was soft.

"Isao was on Saipan," Mr. Nishiyama said. "When we lost there, most of the surviving soldiers came to Okinawa. I keep hoping to discover that's where he is."

A small sliver of hope is all he has, I thought. Gorou told us when Saipan fell, over thirty thousand Japanese soldiers died. What were the chances that Mr. Nishiyama's son survived that slaughter? I didn't voice my thoughts; what benefit was it to tear the fragile fabric of hope?

After dinner that night, Mama wrote to Yumiko; she also had Harumi and me add our thoughts to the letter. I spent a long time thinking about what I would write. I sometimes felt words of sympathy seemed to be elegant, but empty. I didn't want to create that impression. I wanted Yumiko to understand clearly how Mamoru's presence had been an important part of my life. Finally, I decided to describe an incident from when I was five.

When I was little, Mamoru frightened me. He never spoke much, and when he did, his voice was gruff. That didn't stop me from following him and Papa whenever they worked in the barn.

One day, after Papa showed me how to milk the cow, I decided to milk her on my own. This was the cow we owned before Gentle Lady, and she wasn't gentle at all. I had just set the milking stool next to her back leg and was about to sit down when an arm grabbed me and pulled me away—seconds before the cow's leg kicked the stool across the barn.

Mamoru snatched me from danger. He stood me on my feet out of the cow's reach, straightened my clothes, and said something about learning the difference between good intentions and foolishness. That day I learned Mamoru, underneath his rough voice, cared for me and I began to care for him. Later, when Papa told me we know people by their actions, I understood exactly what he meant—Mamoru had already taught me.

We finished Yumiko's letter, and the next day, I walked into town to mail it. I gave the envelope to Mrs. Higa and watched as she put it in the basket. I didn't know if Yumiko would receive it soon, or ever. I hoped that all the thoughts and feelings we had for her and Mamoru somehow reached her and were a comfort, even if the letter was never delivered. Mama always spoke about the power of ancestral spirits; now would be a fine time for them to contribute to our lives in a beneficial way.

November passed into December, and we fell into a comfortable wintertime routine. I don't know how he did it, but somehow Uncle Hiroshi acquired a supply of kerosene. He never said, but I suspected Gorou was involved in the transaction. Since I hadn't seen him for over a month and Uncle Hiroshi was closed-mouth, all I had was my suspicion. However, it was wonderful to have kerosene. It became dark soon after five o'clock in the winter; without fuel for the lamps, the nights would be terribly long.

Under the soft glow of the lanterns, we gathered in Uncle Hiroshi's and Aunty Maiko's room after dinner each evening. Aunty Maiko set up her sewing machine and, with the fabric that she brought with her when she moved in with us, taught Harumi and me how to sew. Rather, she attempted to teach me how to sew. It didn't take long for me, and poor Aunty Maiko, to realize I had no immediate talent. Between stepping on the treadle, watching how I pushed the material under the needle, and trying to make even stitches, I ended up with hours spent ripping out the mangled disasters I created in a few minutes of sewing. Aunty Maiko, not willing to give up, had me practice with no thread. She even tried using paper with lines drawn on it for me to follow. It didn't matter; I was a failure on every level. The only consolation I had was the fact that Mama declared herself a "failed seamstress" also. She said she was too impatient to learn, and the only sewing she did was minor repairs.

Much to Mama's and my surprise, Harumi became Aunty Maiko's star pupil. It only took a short time for her to develop the necessary rhythm of the wheel and the treadle while she guided cloth under the bobbing needle.

"This is fun," Harumi said. "I don't understand why you are having problems, Atsuko. You just line everything up, push the wheel, and pedal."

"Maybe fun for you," I said. "When I try, nothing moves in the right direction."

"Well, I like it," Harumi said. "Aunty Maiko, what should we make? Can we use silk?"

"You are doing very well, but I don't think you are quite ready for silk." Aunty Maiko laughed at Harumi's enthusiasm. "First, we will use heavy cotton. Hiroshi needs new work pants." Aunty Maiko left the room and returned a few minutes later, carrying a bolt of white material. "We are fortunate to have this cotton. It's from India. I bought it several years ago. It's impossible to find material of this quality anymore."

"What do people use then?" Harumi asked.

"A cloth called *sufu*," said Aunty Maiko. "It's made of small amounts of cotton woven with wood pulp and tree bark."

"Sounds uncomfortable." Harumi made a face. "I wouldn't want to wear underwear made from tree bark."

"I tried sewing with *sufu* once." Aunty Maiko shook her head. "The fabric wasn't very soft, and even worse, it tore easily. It would make poor work clothes." Aunty Maiko showed Harumi how to make a pattern and cut the material for Uncle Hiroshi's new pants.

While they were busy measuring and cutting, I decided to work on my own project. When I was eight years old, Papa gave me a blue notebook and suggested I start a Book of Days. I could fill the blank pages with anything I wanted to write about my daily life. At first, I practiced writing my name, over and over, trying to draw the symbols that represented Atsuko perfectly. Then I worked on the family name, Oshiro. Mama told me the name *Atsuko* had several meanings.

The *ko* part meant "child," and my name meant "warm child, honest child," or the meaning I liked best, "kind child." The way to draw *kind child* was 篤子. *Oshiro* meant "large castle," drawn as 大城. The rest of that first notebook was filled with simple drawings and stories I copied from other books. I didn't fully understand I should be writing my own thoughts and observations.

Every year, at New Year's, Papa gave me a new Book of Days. He told me I had a gift for language, and my notebooks were a private place where I could express myself. After he died, Mama carried on the tradition, and I continued to receive new books to fill. Sadly, I had been so busy with farmwork; my Book of Days became a Book of Once in a While. With the arrival of winter, my life became less hectic; I could devote time to the book for 1944. Looking back, I saw my last entry was written the day after Sayuri left Iejima. So much happened since then, how could I best describe the past seven months?

I wrote for several hours, chronicling recent events. When I read over what I had written, it seemed to be impersonal. Somehow, my words didn't convey the emotions I experienced through all the hardships we endured. Or my mixed feelings about Gorou. I thought about it for a while, and ended the entry with this reflection:

> We Oshiros are farmers. The land has been in our family for many years. To be successful, we control our animals, plant crops, and nurture both. Even though we are still farmers, the circumstances of war have removed our ability to determine the course of our lives. We have no animals and cannot even determine the fate of our crops. Everyone is suffering this same lack of freedom and prosperity. Not only does Japan suffer from severe shortages, the conditions are so extreme it is hard to live an honorable life. I'm afraid all these hardships may destroy the souls of the Japanese people. How are we to survive, even

if we live beyond the war? With so much destruction around me, should I even plan a future?

I ended with a haiku.

Winter nights, long, dark.
The moon, hidden behind clouds,
I have lost my way.
Atsuko Oshiro

Chapter 14

December contained one of my favorite traditions, *Touji*, and my mood lightened as we began to prepare for the celebration of the winter solstice. I used to wonder why we found joy in the shortest, and usually the gloomiest, day of the year. When I asked Papa about it, he explained how *Touji* was a hopeful time for us; it meant the days would become longer, and the growing season was once again returning.

In order to observe the day properly, we needed a fruit and a vegetable—*yuzu* and *kabocha*. Luckily, we had plenty of both. Our *yuzu* tree, growing alongside the peanut field, had produced an abundance of the round, yellow fruit. While they were too sour to eat like an orange, they did add zest when a little was used in a vegetable dish or soup. However, that was not how we used them on the night of *Touji*. Floating on the water, *yuzu* were part of our bath.

Mama said a *yuzu* bath prevented us from catching cold during the winter, and the strong fragrance of the fruit removed evil from our bodies and purified them. The truth was that a bath with *yuzu* smelled good, and afterward, my skin felt smooth. I was glad Mama said we would continue to observe this custom.

In the past year, our bathing habits changed. Faced with a shortage of wood and charcoal to heat the water, we no longer bathed every evening as we used to. For a family who worked in the fields, this was a difficult adjustment. We washed ourselves daily, but we didn't soak in the large wooden tub very often. Earlier in the fall, bathing became a topic of discussion between Mama and Uncle Hiroshi.

"Sometimes I wonder about the wisdom of our leaders." Uncle Hiroshi removed the headphones from the radio and shook his head at what he heard. He joined Mama and me as we walked out to the barn one evening. "The speaker announced that no matter how severe the shortages, the people of Japan will never have to endure the closing of the *sento*."

"What else did he say?" Mama asked.

"The government in Tokyo has stated that the public baths are too important for the Japanese, and they must be kept open, under all circumstances."

"Only people with status and money use the *sento*," Mama said. "It seems keeping them open is not very considerate. Think of all the people who have nothing."

"I agree," Uncle Hiroshi said. "Sadly, we were not consulted on the matter."

"We may not bathe as we used to, but we will have *yuzu* baths in December," Mama said. "Somehow, we will find the fuel."

"We have that dead tree." Uncle Hiroshi made a gesture in the general direction of where an old, gnarled apple tree stood silhouetted against the setting sun.

"No, Hiroshi, we will not cut that tree down." Mama spoke slowly, separating her words.

"I didn't mean to wake your dragon." Uncle Hiroshi stepped back and held his hands up, as though surrendering. "Why do you forbid it?"

"That tree used to be fruitful. Each fall it was heavy with apples, some of the most delicious I've ever eaten. We enjoyed those apples until 1924, when a blight attacked the tree, and it has been dead ever since."

"And you've never chopped it down?"

"The poor tree met its fate the same month as my Daiki succumbed to scarlet fever."

I was surprised to hear this. Mama seldom spoke of Daiki, an older brother I never knew. He died two years before I was born and existed only as a name on the scroll hanging in the alcove, along with other family members who had died.

"I understand," Uncle Hiroshi said. "The tree stands for more than just itself."

"Not only that," Mama said. "I did try to chop it down, but I couldn't get close enough. When I held the axe and approached the trunk, invisible hands pushed me away. To all outward appearances, that tree has no life, but it is inhabited by a forceful spirit."

"Don't worry." Uncle Hiroshi put a hand on Mama's shoulder. "I will not try to take an axe to the old tree."

"We will look in the woods by the lake instead," Mama said. "We cannot chop down any trees there, but we can take the fallen branches and twigs."

That wasn't a new idea. We had been going frequently to the woods on the other side of the lake, searching for fuel. We also walked down the gulch that led to Iwa Cove. Whenever we went to either place, we were not alone. Our neighbors joined us; we were all scavengers who scoured the countryside for scraps to fill empty woodboxes.

The other way we celebrated the winter solstice was eating *kabocha*, the squash we harvested in great amounts at the end of October. They didn't have much flavor if we ate them right after we cut them from the vines. Instead, we kept the dark-green squash in a warm place for two weeks. While they sat in the warmth, they ripened, and their flavor changed. After that, we moved them to the coolness of the root cellar to finish turning into smooth, sweet vegetables. The squash were not only delicious; they lasted in storage for several months. Mama said *kabocha* were auspicious—eating them on the winter solstice would bring us luck in the coming year. She also told us, as part of our meal, they would protect us from colds and strokes. While I appreciated that *kabocha* were lucky and healthy, I liked them for their sweet taste, and we could eat them for most of the winter.

And so we celebrated *Touji*. We emerged, fresh and sweet smelling from our *yuzu* baths, followed by a feast of rice and a vegetable stew that included *kabocha*, of course.

Soon after our *Touji* feast, Mama sent us into action—preparing for New Year's. The entire house was to be spotless, and Mama designated a job for all of us. We each wore a *kappogi* to protect our clothing. Mama even found an old one left by Yumiko that Uncle

Hiroshi could use. Although Yumiko was taller than Mama, her apron didn't quite fit Uncle Hiroshi; but he managed to tie it behind his back. He did look out of place—with his arms hanging too far out of the sleeves—wielding a mop and bucket.

The five of us swept, dusted, and washed; it didn't take long to bring our house in order. Under Mama's direction, no corner was left untouched. We even organized and cleaned the root cellar.

"We work too quickly." Harumi brushed a stray hair out of her face and left a streak of dirt across her forehead. "We should slow down, or Mama will have us scrubbing the barns."

"But our house looks wonderful now," I said. "The new year will start the way it should—a clean beginning. When we remove all the dirt of this year, it's as though we have rid ourselves of all the old problems and obstacles that have crept into our lives." I looked at my sister's smudges and rubbed my face, wondering if I had the same smears.

"You just made it worse." Harumi's observation confirmed my suspicion. "But look at Aunty Maiko. It's not fair."

Our aunt emerged from her room where she had been on her hands and knees, scrubbing the wooden floor. She looked as tidy as she had before she began working. I didn't understand it; Aunty Maiko worked as hard as anyone, and yet she never looked disheveled. No dirt clung to her face, not a hair was out of place, even her apron looked untouched.

Aunty Maiko looked at us and laughed. "What are you looking at, nieces?"

"It's just like the peanut field, Aunty Maiko, you are not messed up at all," Harumi said.

"I've had long years of practice. When I worked as a seamstress, we were expected to keep our work and our appearances neat, no matter what. It wasn't easy to learn, but now it's habit."

After she said that, both Harumi and I tried to stay tidy as we worked. We were successful—for a short time. However the longer we cleaned, we lapsed back into our careless methods and became just as smudged and rumpled as ever.

We completed cleaning our house by the end of December, and much to Harumi's relief, we didn't have to scrub the barn. Mama said we worked hard enough and she was proud of us. She said our efforts must have certainly removed all the evil that had crept into our lives during the past year and we were sure to have an auspicious new year. I hoped she was right because 1944 had not brought us much good fortune.

1945

Chapter 15

New Year's was a time to think ahead, but it was also important to look back. I wrote an entry in my Book of Days about tradition and what Japanese heritage meant to me. I was proud of my culture and its traditions, but sometimes it puzzled me. Papa explained New Year's to me when I was younger. He said that most of Japan celebrated on the first of January, but we observed different traditions. We lived in the Ryukyu Islands, and our New Year celebration began with the first new moon—same as the Chinese New Year. However, in 1945, we observed New Year's twice: Uncle Hiroshi's and Aunty Maiko's New Year, and ours, several weeks later. Harumi said Mama used the two celebrations so we could clean the house twice. Luckily, Mama didn't hear her.

The day before New Year's, Uncle Hiroshi, Harumi, and I decorated the entrance to our house with pine and bamboo to greet the coming year. While we were busy hanging boughs around the door, Mama and Aunty Maiko worked in the kitchen, preparing the special food we would eat. The temple gongs on Iejima didn't ring on the first of January, but we listened to the radio broadcast of the bells rung in Tokyo. One hundred eight times the gongs were struck to atone for the one hundred eight human sins and help rid us of the one hundred eight worldly desires. Then we walked down to Iwa Cove where we stood on the cliff and looked east to see the first sunrise. Afterward, we drank the first water, and made our first wishes for 1945. We did these things to honor the festival on the day that Uncle Hiroshi and Aunty Maiko were accustomed to celebrate it.

"We should visit Mr. Nishiyama today," Mama said after we finished our midday meal. "He is from the north, and this is his New

Year's also. Poor man hasn't heard from his son, and this is not a good day to be alone."

"May I go with you?" Harumi asked.

"We'll all go," Aunty Maiko said.

"Atsuko, can you write a greeting for him?" Mama stood up and gestured to Uncle Hiroshi. "We have plenty of pine boughs and cones we can take to him. Let's gather some together."

Using my best pen, I wrote a brief message on a note card:

> May the new year be an auspicious one and bring you much luck.

We all signed it.

Dressed in our best clothes, the five of us walked to our neighbor's house just to the north of ours. Our farm wasn't very large, but Mr. Nishiyama's was smaller. With his son in the army, along with all the other able-bodied men, he had only himself to work the land. Signs of neglect were evident to us. Large portions of his fields were overgrown, and the only livestock was his aged horse, Hero, standing in a pasture. Our visit surprised Mr. Nishiyama, but he greeted us with dignity, bowing and inviting us into his simple home.

Mr. Nishiyama's house was spotless inside, and he asked us to gather at his table and join him for some tea. After he poured tea into our cups, he bowed to Harumi to indicate that she should pour his. Harumi tried to maintain her poise, but a tiny, pleased smile showed how proud she was to be singled out for this small privilege. After we drank, toasting the New Year and expressing our optimism for it, I gave Mr. Nishiyama the card we all signed.

"I am honored to be remembered this way by your family." Mr. Nishiyama held the card as though it were valuable and read its message several times. Then he walked over to a small table at the side of the room and leaned the card against a vase so it would be displayed. "Thank you for your kindness."

We didn't stay much longer. At the entrance, the five of us put our outside shoes back on and bowed to Mr. Nishiyama. He bowed to each one of us in return and stood at the door watching us leave.

"I think he was glad of our visit," Uncle Hiroshi said as we walked away.

"But didn't you notice?" Aunty Maiko asked. "The poor man has almost nothing."

"True." Mama frowned. "Consider how hard we have worked to have enough food. And we are younger and able to do much more than Mr. Nishiyama."

Harumi looked at me with a question in her eyes. I knew what she asked, and I nodded.

"Why can't we share some of our food with Mr. Nishiyama?" I asked. "We have more than enough. More than we had last winter, and we didn't starve then."

"I agree," Mama said. "We can share our rice and vegetables with Mr. Nishiyama. We'll put together a collection and take it to him. Won't he be surprised when we return so soon."

Back home we organized the food to take to our neighbor. One of the bags of rice, five or six squash, jars of pickled carrots, radishes, and cucumbers were loaded into the pushcart, along with a bag of peanuts we had roasted.

We took turns pushing the cart to Mr. Nishiyama's house. Rolling it down our driveway and along the road was easy, but shoving the cart up his driveway was a challenge. The steep incline was filled with ruts. Harumi, Uncle Hiroshi, and I worked together and moved the cart the final stretch.

Mr. Nishiyama was indeed surprised to see us again. "What may I do for you? Is there a problem?" he asked.

"We would like to impose on your generosity," Mama said. "Would you be so kind as to take these poor items?"

Mr. Nishiyama stood in front of the cart and stared down at its contents for a long moment, saying nothing. Then he looked up at us. He had tears in his eyes.

"A thousand blessings on you," he said. "I have been without anything to eat for several days now and didn't know how I would survive. You have given hope to an old man."

"You have brought good fortune to us many times before," Mama said. "We are glad to repay the favor." Mama bowed to Mr.

Nishiyama, and he returned the gesture. He followed that by bowing repeatedly to all of us. We rolled the cart to the back of Mr. Nishiyama's house and unloaded it. The shelves in his kitchen, which had been bare, looked much better with the bags and jars of food on them. We left, accompanied once again by repeated bows and humble thanks.

Walking back, we were mostly silent. I reflected on the difficulties our elderly neighbor faced. It seemed as though the others were thinking similar thoughts.

As we approached our house, Mama did speak. "Girls, giving food to Mr. Nishiyama was your idea, and I am proud of you."

Mama's rare compliment had the effect of humbling me. I knew my spirit of generosity came from the many examples she set.

The second celebration of New Year's was more elaborate than the one we celebrated a few weeks earlier. Again, we recognized first occasions—more of them than we observed before. We walked down to the cove and looked at the sunrise again, but we also noted the first laughter of the year, the first dream, the first cup of tea, and the first meal. Another significant first, is the first letter. In order to assure the first written message brings good luck, we exchanged *omikugi*—short notes foretelling our fortunes.

Mama made *soba* noodles as part of the special dinner she prepared. We ate them on New Year's because the noodles symbolized a long life. No one expected to have them; they were made of wheat, which had been impossible to buy for a long time. However, Mama hoarded the wheat and hadn't told us so it would be a surprise.

Uncle Hiroshi also had a gift for the family. After dinner, he gave Mama a tin canister filled with wooden matches. The matches were not as splendid as other presents we had received in previous years, but they proved to be precious. We needed them to cook and light our lamps, but the government was limiting them to three a day for each family. Most of the time, we couldn't even obtain that many. We had resorted to using an old flint striker. It didn't always work and, even with the best results, required time and effort.

The final part of our celebration was the letter exchange. Each one of us had drawn the name of a person we'd give a slip of paper with their fortune written on it. These could be good wishes or curses. Of course no one made a curse, and all the hopes for the coming year were for a favorable future. After we unfolded the red slips of paper and read the contents, we shared the messages and left the notes lying open on the table to invite the outcomes into our home.

Mama's fortune: 末小吉 (future blessings)
Aunty Maiko's fortune: 方角 (auspicious direction)
Uncle Hiroshi's fortune: 大吉 (great blessing)
Harumi's fortune: 願事 (one's wishes or desires to be fulfilled)
My fortune: 學問 (Success with studies or learning)

With all those good wishes, and the family safely together, I hoped the coming year lived up to our dreams of a better future. Unfortunately, the demons of war had other plans for us.

Chapter 16

A few days after we celebrated the arrival of 1945, my optimism for the future began to unravel. The Americans dropped firebombs on Tokyo and destroyed large sections of the city. We listened to broadcasts from our capital describing the attacks until the radio station ceased operating. Then we had to receive news from Osaka or Nagoya. Since their stations did not send strong signals, it was often difficult to hear the reports. By the time Tokyo's station returned to power, another battle was in progress.

American troops landed on Iwo Jima, and according to our leaders, "the Japanese are prepared to defend the island with honor and will not surrender." The day we learned about Iwo Jima, Uncle Hiroshi went to the village pier in an attempt to buy a fish. He was unsuccessful in his quest, but he did talk with a sergeant he knew. According to the officer, the soldiers returning from Saipan came back in horrible shape, with most of them on the brink of starvation. It was disheartening to realize these poor men were expected to fight to the death on Iwo Jima. I didn't know how they could withstand the force of the Americans. My concern was short-lived, however, as our family's problems suddenly worsened.

We celebrated New Year's on a Tuesday, and on the following Saturday afternoon, two military officers came to our door. They showed little respect when they entered our house. No polite bows were exchanged, and they continued to wear their muddy boots, even on the *tatami* mats in the dining room. Without acknowledging Mama, the older officer handed Uncle Hiroshi a letter. When he opened it, I caught a glimpse of an official-looking seal at the top.

Uncle Hiroshi spent a few minutes reading the message, frowning at its contents.

"Surely the army doesn't—" Uncle Hiroshi started to respond.

"It will not do any good to protest," the warrant officer said. "The decision is final."

"What does the letter say?" Mama spoke for the first time.

"It's from General Kawabe. He writes 'the Oshiro farm has been given the privilege to become an air base for the Japanese Imperial forces.'" Uncle Hiroshi swallowed before continuing. "It goes on to say, 'The family has been granted two weeks to vacate.' We can take personal belongings—as much as each person can carry. We are expected to report at the ferry landing by noon on the third of March. The military will transport us to a camp on Okinawa."

"N—" Harumi started to protest, and Aunty Maiko, who stood next to her, clamped her hand across Harumi's mouth. Harumi jerked her head free, turned, and rushed out of the room, leaving the house by the back door.

"You have read the orders and repeated them. It is clear that you understand the message." The officer spoke in clipped tones. "We will take possession of this farm in two weeks. If you have not left, you will be forcibly removed and denied the opportunity to take any of your belongings."

The two soldiers left as abruptly as they arrived. Again, they did not bow. Instead, they clicked their heels, turned, and marched out. They rode off in a car driven by a third soldier.

Uncle Hiroshi handed Mama the letter. She knelt at the table and read it.

"Maiko, would you prepare some tea?" Mama looked up at us after she finished reading. "We need to discuss our latest catastrophe. Atsuko, will you go after Harumi and bring her back?"

I found Harumi sitting on the back steps, holding Miss Singer.

"Can't we just refuse to leave?" Harumi asked.

"You left before the soldier explained," I said. "It will be much worse if we don't follow orders. Come in now. Mama wants to talk with us."

Harumi let go of the cat, and Miss Singer ran off to the barn. We stood, but before we turned to go inside, I saw Gorou walking up the path next to the barn—the trail that came from Iwa Cove. Harumi went into the house while I waited on the steps for Gorou. More than three months had passed since I talked to Gorou, and I was nervous about seeing him. I thought about him—a lot. I imagined he regretted his words to me and lost interest. However, my apprehension faded when he reached the porch, and he followed his brief bow with a warm smile.

"I saw the soldiers leave your house." Gorou's expression became serious. "Is your farm in danger?"

"Yes."

"I heard the military intended to take farmland on our island. What did they tell you?"

"Come in the house with me. Mama wants to talk about our dilemma."

"Will I be intruding?"

"Gorou, you have helped us so many times before, I'm sure everyone will appreciate your presence."

"Maybe I can be useful again."

The dread that had washed over me lessened with the relief I felt at Gorou's offer to help us. We joined the rest of the family gathered at the table where Aunty Maiko poured tea.

After everyone's cup was filled, Mama spoke, "I never considered this would happen. How can we be expected to...?"

"You heard what the officer said," Uncle Hiroshi said. "We have no choice."

"No." Mama rose and faced the shrine. No one said anything while Mama had her back to us. Then she took a deep breath and turned around. "This farm has been in the Oshiro family for over two hundred years—since Japan was ruled by the *shoguns*. First, my girls lost their school. Next, the soldiers took our animals. We were required to give away most of our crops. Now we are to leave our home? How can I let this happen? I cannot express loyalty to both our ancestors and the government anymore." Mama came back to the table and knelt down next to me.

"Won't the family be together in the camp?" Aunty Maiko spoke in a soft voice.

"I have heard conditions in the camps are horrible," Mama said. "Mrs. Higa has described what her sister's family suffered. We will be surrounded by filth and disease. Atsuko and Harumi will not be safe—terrible indignities are forced upon young girls."

"Would it be better if we refuse to leave and the soldiers shoot us in our home?" Uncle Hiroshi asked.

"Did the soldiers say they would kill us?" Harumi's voice went up several notes in alarm.

"I'm pretty sure that is what they meant by 'forcibly removed and not taking any belongings,'" Uncle Hiroshi said.

"Two choices—go or stay." Mama held up three fingers. "Let's consider a third option."

"What are you thinking?" I asked.

"Hiroshi, we grew up on Okinawa. What do you remember about the cliffs?"

"I remember the trails along the cliffs of the northwest corner," Uncle Hiroshi said. "We knew them so well we could walk the edges blindfolded." He paused. "Are you thinking of the caves?"

"Yes." Mama nodded her head. "I'm sure we could find a suitable one—as I recall, there were many."

"If you want to use a cave on Okinawa, the northwest corner of the island would be safest." Gorou spoke for the first time. "Japanese soldiers are stationed in the south, but large sections of the north are deserted."

"It is fortuitous. We know the northwest, and it is the safest area," Mama said. "We must think of how to find the best cave."

"Let me help," Gorou said. "I have been up and down the coast of Okinawa many times. I can take you on a search for your new home."

"You can take us on your boat?" Mama asked.

"Yes. Luckily, we are north of town, and we want to cross the water north of the ferry landing. If we leave early, we should be able to reach Okinawa without being stopped."

"Wait, I'll be right back." Mama stood up and left the room. She returned a few minutes later with a rolled-up map. With it spread out on the table, Gorou pointed to the route he would take with Mama and Uncle Hiroshi to search for a suitable cave. From the northeast corner of Iejima, they would go east across the East China Sea and follow the coast of Okinawa past Kouri Island until they reached an area where very few people lived.

While Mama, Uncle Hiroshi, and Gorou talked about their plans for the next day, Aunty Maiko talked to Harumi and me. "While they look for a place, we can start to prepare for the move. We must decide what is essential."

"Miss Singer!" Harumi turned to Mama. "We have to take Miss Singer. She's essential—she's worked hard all year keeping our food protected. Please say we can take her."

"Miss Singer should be able to go with us," Mama said. "But I don't know how we can move her safely—cats don't like water."

"I will build her a crate," Uncle Hiroshi said. "After we arrive, we can use the wood. It will be a box with two purposes."

"Do you think she will stay with us?" I asked.

"Of course she will," Harumi said. "Miss Singer loves us."

"I think that is an exaggeration as far as cats are concerned," Aunty Maiko said. "But I know a trick to convince her to remain with us."

"What is it? What is your cat trick?" Harumi asked. "It won't hurt her, will it?"

"*Yare*, nothing such as that." Aunty Maiko laughed. "When we are ready to open the crate, we rub fish oil on Miss Singer's paws and legs. By the time she has washed herself, she'll be ready to settle down. She'll think of her new home as a place with plenty of fish."

"Harumi will bring her cat, I will bring our shrine," Mama said. "In addition to food and supplies, each of us can bring something that is a personal choice."

I reached up and felt the small elephant Sayuri gave me the last time I saw her. Of course it would go with me, but I hoped it wouldn't count as my personal choice. "I would like to bring my desk, with a few books and my writing materials." I had a portable desk Papa made for me when I was ten. It was a wooden box with a hinged lid that slanted. Inside I kept paper, pens, and my Book of Days. I even had room for my book of poems from Sister Dominica.

"Your desk is a good choice," Mama said. "Hiroshi, what do you want to bring?"

"My books," he said. "Not all of them—the ones I like to reread. They are old friends."

I was glad Uncle Hiroshi picked books. Since he moved to the farm, he encouraged me to read from his collection. We spent many evenings discussing not only Japanese authors such as Natsume, but also translations of Western classics. He owned several books by Dickens. I remember being surprised to learn about the struggles of poor people on the other side of the world. I wondered if the people in England had a chance to learn about our Japanese culture.

"Maiko, what do you want to bring?" Mama asked. "Your dolls?"

"No, not the dolls. I do hope we can find a safe place to store everything we don't take with us." Aunty Maiko swept her arm around the room to indicate the furniture and wall hangings. "I would like us to have nice clothing, along with our work clothes. We may not live in a house, but we don't need to lose our manners. I will look after our dress attire."

"Gorou, you haven't spoken for a while," Mama said. "Are we requesting too much? Will it be a burden? After all, we cannot move without your help."

Gorou bowed his head in acknowledgment of Mama's concern. "You can bring as much as we can manage in my boat for as long as I have fuel and we aren't arrested."

"You are very generous," Mama said.

"In the past I benefitted from the kindness of your family," Gorou said. "It is only right that I return that kindness, and I may need your help. You are not the only people who face an uncertain future. My situation has grown more perilous in the past few months—I've been staying away from Iejima. I may have to impose on you to escape danger."

Two thoughts raced through my brain when Gorou spoke of recent trouble. Fear that Gorou would experience a terrible fate and relief that he hadn't been avoiding me. Strange to think that bad news could somehow be comforting. Strange and a little selfish. In my mind, I criticized myself.

"What will we do with everything we cannot take?" Uncle Hiroshi asked. "Do we leave our belongings for the soldiers to find?"

"No," Mama said. "We will leave nothing. I have an idea. They won't want Mr. Nishiyama's land for an airstrip. It's too steep. We can ask him to keep what's left in one of his barns."

It was decided that when Gorou took Mama and Uncle Hiroshi the next day, Aunty Maiko, Harumi, and I would walk to Mr. Nishiyama's and ask him if we could use one of his barns. Then we would spend the rest of the day organizing our belongings.

Uncle Hiroshi went to his room to look over his books while Mama, Aunty Maiko, and Harumi went to pick out clothes. I planned to take the tea things to the kitchen and clean up, but since Gorou lingered at the table, I remained, kneeling across from him.

"I didn't want to be gone this long," Gorou said. "Iejima had become unsafe for me."

"What happened?"

"My friends warned me about a certain sergeant. I was safe as long as he thought I was an idiot, but he grew suspicious when he overheard me tell a fisherman how to fix his boat. Then my friends left Iejima, and I had no one I could trust."

"What friends? And why did they leave?"

"My friends in the army. The supply sergeant I traded with and the corporal who gave me information."

"Where are they now?"

"The corporal was transferred. He's fighting on Iwo Jima. The supply sergeant was arrested for trading on the black market."

"Was he trading with you?"

"Not when he was arrested. He was trying to obtain medicine for his daughter from someone who calls himself Mr. Black. He's also known as the Black Pirate."

"It could have been you." I shivered, thinking about Gorou falling into the hands of the Economic Police.

"I hope I have been smarter than they were. The two met in front of the post office, and a military car was parked nearby. The police arrested Mr. Black first. When he gave information against my friend, the pirate was set free, and my friend was executed."

I shivered again at the brutality of the police. Then I remembered what Uncle Hiroshi told us about the battle on Iwo Jima. "The corporal faces a certain death too. What's worse, the sergeant standing before a firing squad or the corporal fighting until he's killed?" I reached over and grabbed Gorou's hand. "I'm glad nothing like that happened to you."

"That's why I might have to ask your family for refuge. I need to stay invisible."

"Will it be dangerous? Taking Mama and Uncle Hiroshi to Okinawa?"

"Not if we leave early. I know the routes of the Navy—they are south of the ferry passage. We will avoid them. So far, the military hasn't interfered with the fishermen around here." Gorou gave my hand a squeeze and stood up. "Your mama said I could stay in the empty cottage. I need to bring my gear from the boat and settle in before dinner."

"Dinner! I still need to clean the kitchen." Gorou left, and I grabbed the cups we used for tea just as Mama walked down the hall, headed to the kitchen to cook our dinner.

That night, we talked for a long time after our evening meal. As horrible as it was to learn we were about to lose our home, the plan we devised to escape two dismal choices gave our family a sense of hope. It was the animation that comes with a purpose and a goal. The realization our success depended on what we accomplished in the next two weeks was also a little frightening. Could the six of us survive when hundreds of thousands of Japanese perished?

Chapter 17

On Sunday, Gorou took Mama and Uncle Hiroshi to find a suitable cave for our new home. All six of us walked down to Iwa Cove, three of us to send the three adventurers on their quest. The night sky had just begun to fade into morning gray when we reached Gorou's boat. The water of the East China Sea lapped quietly against the rocks; it appeared to be a good day for their trip. With the three travelers on board, Harumi and I pushed the boat away from shore. Gorou lowered the engine's propeller into the water, and after a few pulls, the engine roared to life. We stood on the beach for a few minutes and watched the boat as it headed east toward Okinawa, leaving a trail of widening waves.

"Do you think they will find a place?" Harumi yawned as we started our walk back up the hill. "I hope so. I don't want to live in a camp."

"Mama seemed hopeful last night," I said. "And you know Mama—when she puts her mind to something, she usually succeeds."

"While they are cave hunting, what are we going to do today?" Harumi asked.

"*Yare*, we will be very busy," Aunty Maiko said. "It's good our day is starting early."

"What should we do first? Go visit Mr. Nishiyama?" Harumi liked to go to his farm so she could spend time with Hero.

"It's far too early to visit Mr. Nishiyama," Aunty Maiko said. "We'll go in the afternoon. If we work on organizing the household first, we'll have a better idea of what we hope to put in storage."

"Do you think he'll keep our things at his farm?" I didn't really think he'd refuse; Mr. Nishiyama was always very polite.

"Arisu suggested I make a business arrangement with him," Aunty Maiko said.

That made sense to me; Mama didn't like to impose on people. More than once she told us people need to rely on themselves, and it was more honorable to help others than to be someone who needed help. "What's the business arrangement?" I asked.

"I am going to insist on paying rent for the space we use," Aunty Maiko said. "I will offer to pay in money and food."

"That's good," I said. "Ever since we visited last month, I've worried about him."

"We all have," Aunty Maiko said. "Your mother even talked about taking him with us, but he won't leave his home as long as he thinks there is a chance his son will return. We have money we can share from the sale of our tobacco. Money isn't very useful right now, but maybe Mr. Nishiyama will have an opportunity to buy supplies. We won't be able to eat all our food before it spoils. We have squash, peanuts, and carrots to offer him. The bag of rice we gave him in January should last for a while yet."

I began to feel better about asking Mr. Nishiyama to store our belongings. Maybe there was a part of Mama in me.

"I'm glad we're going to help Mr. Nishiyama," Harumi said.

I realized Mama's ideas about honor lived in my sister also.

Back at the house, we went through each room to decide what would go with us and what would go into storage.

"Atsuko, will you make a list of the things we need?" Aunty Maiko asked.

I picked up paper and pencil and began to write down what we should take. We each identified items we thought were essential, and the list became lengthy in a very short time.

"This isn't going to work." Aunty Maiko looked over my shoulder and saw how much I wrote. "Let's look again and eliminate much of it. Think in terms of 'necessity.' Otherwise, poor Gorou will need to make endless trips in his boat."

As we went back over the list and crossed off most of it, a sudden realization hit me. I always thought of our family as not having many belongings, and probably, compared to many others, we didn't own that much. However, after whittling down the list to just the necessities and seeing what was left, I noticed we had surrounded ourselves with a surprising number of possessions. We would be taking far more to Mr. Nishiyama for storing than would be going with us to Okinawa. Then another thought sprang to mind—how much worse it would be if we followed orders and only took what we could carry. The life we worked so hard to build for ourselves would be completely destroyed.

After lunch, the three of us walked to Mr. Nishiyama's house. Hero grazed next to the fence bordering the driveway and lifted his head as we approached. We stopped for a few moments while Harumi said hello to the horse and fed him the apple she brought with her. The old horse nodded as if to thank Harumi for the treat while she talked to him in a low voice.

"That apple Harumi sneaked from the house will be payment in advance if Hero is put to work hauling for us." Aunty Maiko smiled at me; she turned to Harumi. "We're moving on. You can stay with Hero for a little while, but don't linger too long."

Mr. Nishiyama stood on his porch to greet us. "Ladies, I am honored that you have come to my house." He bowed, as usual. "Please come inside and join me for some tea."

I helped our elderly neighbor prepare tea in his kitchen and carried the teapot to the dining room. Meanwhile, Harumi had come inside, and the three of us knelt around the table to enjoy Mr. Nishiyama's hospitality.

"It is a pleasure to have your company," Mr. Nishiyama said. "But I think you are here for more than a social visit."

"You are correct." Aunty Maiko nodded. "My sister-in-law sent us to arrange some business with you."

Aunty Maiko explained our predicament to Mr. Nishiyama, how we were in danger of losing everything, along with our farm, and Mama's plan to avoid the government's orders.

"I am sorry such trouble has come to you," Mr. Nishiyama said. "When I was at the post office yesterday, I heard rumors about a farm being taken for an airfield. At the time, I was relieved to think my place unsuitable because of its hills. Now I am ashamed to think my fortune is my good neighbors' misfortune."

"Don't berate yourself." Aunty Maiko reached over to touch Mr. Nishiyama's arm. "Life is such a struggle now, we are all anxious to protect ourselves. Maybe you will be able to help us. As I said, it would be a business arrangement beneficial to you and our family."

We spent the next few minutes describing the "necessities" we planned to take and how we needed to find a place to store our remaining possessions.

"Say no more." Mr. Nishiyama held up his hand. "The place to keep your belongings is here, with me. One of my barns hasn't been used for several years. It is dry and can be locked. I will consider it a privilege if you make use of the space."

"Only if you accept payment—we insist. Along with your barn, we need to rent Hero and your wagon. We hope that you will find our offer acceptable." Aunty Maiko went on to explain how we would like to give him a combination of money and food.

"Weeks ago you saved me with your generosity, and now, even with all your hardships, you save me again." Mr. Nishiyama's eyes filled with tears. "The use of an empty barn is a small inconvenience for what you propose to give me."

We left shortly afterward, escorted to the door by Mr. Nishiyama, who bowed repeatedly to us while we stood on his porch, saying good-bye.

At home, we spent the rest of the day sorting and organizing.

"We need to consider Hero," Aunty Maiko said. "He's willing and patient, but he's also old. We should distribute the heavy furniture in separate trips so he doesn't have to take it all at once."

"I should be the one who drives the wagon," Harumi said. "I'm not heavy."

"You are the best person to help with Hero." Aunty Maiko laughed. "But you can't give him all our apples and carrots—just a few."

Aunty Maiko and I just started dinner when Harumi shouted to us from the entryway. The three searchers were returned from Okinawa.

"What did you find?"

"Did you locate a good cave?"

"Did you have any trouble?"

We all talked at once, until Uncle Hiroshi put up his hand. "If you are quiet, we can tell you about our adventures."

"Atsuko, will you prepare tea for us?" Mama asked. "We'll have something to drink, and you can learn about our day."

While I was in the kitchen making tea, I wondered about the trip to Okinawa. Mama's expression didn't reveal whether the news was good or bad, but Uncle Hiroshi laughed when he asked us to be quiet. *Oh well,* I thought, *I'll find out soon enough.*

I returned to the dining room with the tea, and nothing important was discussed while Aunty Maiko poured our tea and I passed the rice cakes.

"The trip today revived so many memories of when we were young," Mama said after she had taken a few sips of her tea. "Don't you agree, Hiroshi?"

Uncle Hiroshi nodded, but before he could reply, Harumi spoke.

"Mama, tell us. Don't keep us in suspense any longer."

"Gorou, will you explain where you took us?" Mama asked.

"We went east along the shore of Okinawa until we reached the point opposite Kouri Island. We went around the point and looked for a suitable spot to stop."

"How did you know you'd find caves?" Harumi asked.

"The cliffs of Okinawa are like Iejima, riddled with caves," Uncle Hiroshi said. "It would be hard to find places without them." He nodded at Gorou to continue.

"I landed the boat at an inlet where a small creek flows into it. It's quiet and secluded."

"After securing the boat, we walked along the creek until we found a break in the undergrowth and climbed up a sort of path, until we reached a ledge," Mama said.

"At first we thought we'd pushed our way through the brush up to the only section of cliff on Okinawa without a cave." Uncle

Hiroshi shook his head. "But that's good—the entrance is so hidden it is almost impossible to find."

"So that is where we will be going?" I asked.

"We looked around to see if it would be suitable," Gorou said.

"It's fortunate a creek is nearby, isn't it?" Aunty Maiko asked.

"Yes," said Mama. "But that's not all. We climbed to the top of the cliff and discovered an abandoned farm not far away."

"Why couldn't we stay there?" Harumi asked. "It would be more comfortable than a stinky old cave."

"Not this farm, niece." Uncle Hiroshi frowned at my sister. "The buildings have collapsed with rot. Living there would be impractical and make us too visible. But the farm offers us some good fortune. It has a well with a working pump."

"And open land," Mama said. "I've saved seeds from this year's crop. Maybe we can grow food."

"Grow food?" Harumi asked. "How long are we going to be in a cave?"

"No one can predict what will happen in the war," Aunty Maiko said. "It won't hurt to plan ahead. Tell us, what is the cave like?"

"The ledge is about four feet wide, and a large rock and bush hide the mouth of the cave," Uncle Hiroshi said.

"How big is it?" I asked.

"The opening is small," Uncle Hiroshi said. "You will have to bend over in order to enter."

"What about inside?" Aunty Maiko said. "We aren't bringing many things, but we need space for all of us."

"Not far inside the cave, it's possible to stand, and it divides into two sections. We will fit nicely, and even manage to have a little privacy." Uncle Hiroshi moved his arms to indicate the space overhead and how the cave split.

"What does it smell like?" Harumi asked.

"Not too bad," Mama said. "There must be a small opening in the back, because I felt a draft. That should keep the air fresh." She began to stand. "But I'm hungry after this busy day. I imagine we all are. We should start dinner."

"Aunty Maiko and I were beginning to prepare it when you returned." I gestured at Mama to kneel back down. "We'll make dinner. Harumi will help us while the three of you rest for a while." My aunt and I had planned to put together a simple meal, and luckily, I cooked rice without burning it and added vegetables for an appetizing dinner.

We planned our move all through dinner, lingering at the table longer than usual. Moving our things into storage, we decided, would happen before taking our belongings to the cave.

"Gorou, since you are the expert with the boat, how should we organize the move to Okinawa?" Mama asked.

"From the list, I think I can take everything in three trips," Gorou said. "We will start with the most important. That way, if I'm interrupted, you should have what you need. First, food and kitchen supplies. Second, bedding and clothing. Last, the personal items you picked out."

"And Miss Singer," Harumi said.

"Of course Miss Singer." Gorou smiled. "And when she arrives, her new home will be ready for her."

I was struck by a new fear. "You said 'interrupted' Gorou. What happens if you are stopped?"

"I hope I'm smart enough to avoid anything too disastrous." Gorou smiled reassuringly. "However, we may have to use another strategy."

"What will happen if we are stranded here?" Harumi asked. "Will we have to go to a camp?"

"Our plans would have to go terribly wrong for that to happen," Mama said. "We should be gone from here days before we are expected to leave."

"If for any reason Gorou isn't here to take us, we'll ride the ferry to Okinawa," Uncle Hiroshi said. "So far, people are not being closely watched on the ferries—as long as they travel light."

"Then what?" Harumi's voice shook. "I just know we'll end up in a camp."

"We saw a dirt road leading away from the abandoned farm," Uncle Hiroshi. "It likely goes to Motobu, where the ferry lands. If we find that road, we can walk from the ferry to the cave. It's less than ten miles, and you must remember, we won't be carrying anything with us. See, we have plenty of plans!"

Aunty Maiko and I carried dishes to the kitchen and began cleaning up. Mama went with Harumi to her room; I could hear Mama telling her about the creek and the path up to the cave. By the time I finished in the kitchen, Gorou had left. Uncle Hiroshi walked with him to his sleeping quarters. I was disappointed I hadn't had a chance for a private conversation with Gorou, and I wondered what the two men were talking about in private. *How dangerous will our adventure be?*

That night I thought a long time about what to write in my Book of Days. Much has been taken from us, I thought, and now we choose to leave the rest.

> Autumn strips the leaves,
> yet the tree lives. How much can
> we lose and still live?
> *(Atsuko Oshiro)*

Chapter 18

*In a hidden cove,
we float beneath the mangroves'
sheltering arches.*
—Atsuko Oshiro

We left Iejima on a misty morning eight days after the warrant officer gave us orders to turn our farm over to the military. Uncle Hiroshi went with the first load; his plan was to carry our supplies from the inlet on Okinawa to the cave. Aunty Maiko left next; Mama, Harumi, and I were in the third trip.

As I walked along the path leading to Gorou's boat, I turned around at the crest of the hill before heading down to Iwa Cove and looked back. I was leaving the only home I knew, where for eighteen years I lived with my family and worked in the fields, where Papa and Mama guided and encouraged me. I whispered a little hope for the farm: that it would be safe and we could return someday. Then I murmured a prayer for myself, for whatever lay ahead for my family.

"Do you think we'll ever see our home again?" Harumi looked at me, tears streaming down her face.

"What we are doing will give us the best chance." Even as I spoke, I kept my misgivings to myself—so many terrible events had changed the future for Japan.

"Why didn't we just stay with Mr. Nishiyama? After all, he invited us to move in with him."

"You know what Mama said—if we aren't seen, no one will come looking for us. If we stayed on his farm, we'd be noticeable. And she didn't want us to bring trouble to Mr. Nishiyama either."

In fact, during the time we prepared to leave our home, Mama and Uncle Hiroshi changed our plans considerably. They decided it would look too suspicious if we emptied our house and barns. The only things we stored with our neighbor were Aunty Maiko's doll collection and sewing machine. When the military came to take over, they wouldn't know to look for them, but they would wonder if everything else were gone. "Come on, we need to catch up to Gorou and Mama so we can help load the boat."

The last items we took to the cave were with us in the pushcart, and when we reached Gorou's boat, we moved them onboard. Before he left, Uncle Hiroshi made four crates for us. Mama placed hers—with the house shrine—in a secure spot while Harumi carried a howling Miss Singer in another. Mama's crate was heavier than Harumi's, but wonderfully silent. On the other hand, Miss Singer, who always shared her opinions, started protesting as soon as Harumi confined her and she didn't stop. I had my portable desk and the suitcase with the clothes Aunty Maiko packed. Gorou took charge of the last two crates—the books Uncle Hiroshi chose to save. When we finished moving everything, Gorou took the cart back up the hill and left it in a deserted field.

"Whew." Harumi wrinkled her nose. "Miss Singer should love the way this boat smells—fishy."

"Of course it's fishy—it's a fishing boat." Mama frowned. "Now don't say anything rude in front of Gorou."

When Gorou returned, he arranged our seating before we shoved off. I sat in the bow, while Mama and Harumi occupied the middle seat. Gorou pushed us away from the shore and jumped aboard, all in one move. Using an oar, he maneuvered the boat so we headed out and lowered the propeller. To start the engine, he adjusted several knobs that protruded from the metal casing and wound a cord around the wheel on top. He then pulled the cord in one swift motion. The first time he did this, the engine sputtered, then stopped. It roared to life on the third try, and we were underway—to an uncertain future.

The trip across the East China Sea was uneventful. In the distance I saw the ferry, crossing to Okinawa. Even farther away I spotted two large military ships—ghostly monsters lurking in the mist. Sitting in the front, I faced forward and looked out over the sea, toward the outline of the large island ahead. The noise of the boat's engine blocked all other sound and wrapped me in my own private thoughts. Here we were, gliding over the sea, its secrets held beneath opaque green. *Is that how we travel through our lives? Passing close to a hidden truth, but remaining oblivious?*

After we reached Okinawa and went around a point of land, we didn't see any other boats. Staying close to the shore, we passed an island.

"Kouri Island!" Mama tapped me on the shoulder and shouted into my ear. "It's not far now."

"Good!" I nodded.

Gorou steered the boat even closer to the shoreline. As we approached a small bay, he slowed our speed. We entered a cove; a dense growth of mangrove trees provided a canopy overhead. Gorou cut the engine, and we glided silently into the narrowing inlet. We drifted up next to a grassy ledge where the roots of the mangroves protruded from the ground in gray arches. I had seen mangrove trees all my life, and always thought them spooky. It was as if the visible roots arching downward could start walking, like a huge spider, and the spindly tree would take off on some evil mission. I felt goose bumps when we brushed up next to one.

"Grab a root!" Gorou shouted to me. "Now pull the boat alongside." He jumped out, holding a rope that he tied to the trunk of a tree leaning over the water. "Hand me the rope next to you." With both ropes tied to the tree, the boat was steady against the bank and we could step onto the ledge.

When the three of us were out of the boat, Gorou jumped back in and started to lift out our cargo. He handed a noisy Miss Singer to Harumi.

"You poor baby," Harumi murmured to her cat. "Your terrible boat ride is over. Soon, I'll take you out of this awful cage." Miss Singer responded by sticking a sad little paw through the slats of her crate.

Next came the shrine. Mama put the crate down near the boxes brought over earlier.

"Hiroshi and Maiko have been busy," Mama said. "Almost everything we sent with them must be in the cave already." She pointed to what remained—a few boxes of food and two suitcases.

"Here's your desk." Gorou handed me the wooden box. "And Aunty Maiko's suitcase." He placed it on the grass. "And...the books. Don't lift them—I'll get them." Then Gorou did a surprising thing. He loosened the bolts that held the engine to the boat, lifted it from the stern, and laid it next to the boxes of books. "I'm going to hide the boat, but if anyone finds it, he will be able to steal it. I don't want to lose the engine as well. I worked over two years to pay for it." He reached up and untied the ropes. "I'm taking the boat up to the end of this inlet and hide it in the bushes. I'll be back shortly to carry the heavy things. Don't wait for me."

I looked around the clearing. A path leading to the cave wasn't obvious at first.

"This way." Mama pointed to a clump of bushes, picked up a suitcase, and walked toward the undergrowth. "See these two trees growing close together? Go between them and the bushes." Mama led the way along the mostly hidden path, Harumi and Miss Singer were next, and I followed, carrying my small desk.

At first it didn't seem we were headed to a cliff, let alone a cave. We trudged through dense jungle growth for several minutes. Vines hung down from trees and lay across the ground, where they grabbed our feet if we weren't careful. When we started to climb, the foliage became somewhat sparse. Finally we emerged onto a rocky ledge with a few straggly bushes hugging the cliff.

"You're here!" Aunty Maiko's voice echoed; she was nowhere in sight. "I can hear Miss Singer announcing you." Her words became louder, and then she stepped out from behind one of the rocks. "I'm so glad to see you—safe."

"You've been busy," Mama said. "There's not much more to bring up here."

"That's Hiroshi," Aunty Maiko said. "He carried all the supplies from the first trip to the cave before I arrived. Now he's busy with the shovel."

"He's digging?" Harumi asked. "Why?"

"So we have a toilet." Aunty Maiko smiled at the expression on Harumi's face. "He's down that path." She pointed in the opposite direction from the way we came. "He's making us a fine outdoor accommodation."

"Outdoors?" Harumi said. "That's aw—"

"Harumi—" Mama started to speak.

"Think of it this way," Aunty Maiko interrupted both of them. "If we don't have a toilet, even an outdoor one, we'll have to use a bucket. Someone will be responsible for taking care of the bucket." She looked directly at Harumi when she said that.

"An outdoor toilet—just the thing." Harumi quickly changed the tone of her voice. "Aren't we fortunate?"

"Come inside." Aunty Maiko waved toward the cliff. "You can see what your new house looks like." She led us around the rock next to where she stood and pointed to a small opening.

"That's our cave?" I asked. "It looks so small."

"Don't worry," Mama said. "Inside, it's much bigger—but it is dark."

"I have a lantern burning," Aunty Maiko said. "I needed the light to arrange things."

"Won't we run out of kerosene?" I asked.

"We'll keep the lantern off most of the time," Mama said. "During the day we will be outside—as long as it's safe. At night, we'll be sleeping. Other than that, we'll have to become used to the dark."

I bent over and walked through the opening. Brushing against its sides frightened me, as though the walls would press in on me and I'd stop breathing. I was relieved to discover that not far into the cave, its entrance widened into a room that had enough space to stand. At the far end of this main chamber, two openings branched off in what appeared to be other rooms.

"This will be our common room," Aunty Maiko said. "I put the food and utensils in here. Those are our bedrooms." She pointed to the openings at the back. "I thought the smaller room—on the right—could be for Hiroshi and me. The one on the left is big enough for the three of you."

"Let's look at our room, girls." Mama picked up the lantern and walked into the room Aunty Maiko said was ours.

The room wasn't very large—our three futons had been spread across the floor, leaving only a little extra area. The suitcase holding Harumi's and my clothes stood next to the opening. I was glad to see there was space enough to walk between each futon.

"Do you feel the draft?" Mama asked. "We must be connected to the outside from the back. That's good—it means fresh air."

The cave smelled like dirt, but when Mama said that about fresh air, I realized it didn't smell musty, or even very stale. *Oh well,* I thought, *the smell of dirt is nothing new for a farmer.*

Back in the common room we discussed what to do next. I wanted to bring my desk in, while Harumi was anxious to release Miss Singer.

"Look at this." Mama walked over to a small alcove. "This is a perfect place for our shrine. Having it set up will make this a home."

"Harumi, I think you should leave Miss Singer in the crate for a while so she can become used to this room," Aunty Maiko said. "Atsuko, here is a place for your desk." She indicated a spot next to the alcove where I could keep my writing materials.

"Girls, bring the cat and the desk inside," Mama said. "Then we can go up the hill to the old farm for water. I saw the buckets outside—we'll take them."

"While you go for water, I'll prepare our lunch," Aunty Maiko said. "By the time you return, we will all enjoy a meal and a break."

Once we left the cave, Mama grabbed a bucket and headed toward the path we had just walked up. "This way, girls." Instead of going back down to the inlet, she turned to the left and continued up the cliff. She led us to the top where the path ended on the edge of a field.

"Look back," Mama said. "You want to recognize the way back. See, the path starts by that dead tree."

We walked across the field toward a deserted farmhouse where we found the water pump. While the pump looked like the ones we had at home, it didn't work as smoothly. The arm groaned and was difficult to move. The water it produced had bits of rust in it at first but, after pumping, became clearer. It didn't take very long to fill our buckets and head back down the path. By the time we reached the cave, Aunty Maiko had fixed our lunch. We would be eating out on the ledge. She had turned a crate over, spread a cloth on it, and placed food on the makeshift table. The six of us—Gorou and Uncle Hiroshi had joined us—ate rice mixed with leftover chicken and vegetables. The day before, we butchered the last chicken; and even though it was a poor, skinny bird, Mama and Aunty Maiko planned to use it for several meals.

"Is it time yet to release Miss Singer?" Harumi asked as we finished eating. "She can't stay in her cage forever."

"Yes, but I think you should open her crate inside," Mama said.

"Here, I have something for you." Gorou handed Harumi a small jar. "It's fish oil—for her paws—and a little piece of fish."

"Thank you." Harumi took the jar from Gorou. "Atsuko, will you come with me?"

I nodded, and we went into the cave. "I think you should let her smell the fish before we open the crate," I said. "That way she'll be more interested in the fish than running away."

Harumi opened the jar and dipped her finger in the oil, then stuck it through the slats. "Oh, her tongue is rough." She giggled as Miss Singer licked her finger.

We knelt in front of the crate; I used a hammer's claw to open the box. Harumi lifted the cat out and held her while I spread oil on her paws. I held a piece of fish on my palm and let Miss Singer nibble it. Harumi lowered the cat to the ground, and we watched as Miss Singer licked the fish oil.

When the cat finished cleaning herself, she crawled into Harumi's lap, curled into a ball, and began purring. "It worked," Harumi whispered. "She didn't run away."

I looked down at the animal resting on my sister and thought about the strange new chapter in my life. Maybe survival for my family wasn't an impossible hope.

Chapter 19

It didn't take long for us to settle into a routine, spending our nights in the cave and most of our days outside. We were used to being outdoors; however, the way we occupied our time drastically changed. On the morning of our second day, we sat on the ledge and ate a simple meal of rice cakes and drank tea.

The weather that March was mild. As we relaxed after lunch, I enjoyed the early spring warmth. So far, our days were not like the year before when heavy rains threatened our crops. I remembered when Uncle Hiroshi brought home seeds and the radio in the middle of a torrential downpour. I was glad we could sit in the sun and weren't being driven into the cave by storms.

"You know, people in the United States live like this when they are on vacation. They call it *kyanpu o suro*," Uncle Hirsohi said.

"Americans call living in caves *camping*?" Harumi wrinkled her brow.

"Not in caves, in parks. They use tents and cook over a campfire. Sometimes they hike on trails."

I thought of the parks I had seen in Kyoto and the pictures of city parks in Tokyo. "Don't the police become angry when people damage the landscape? In the middle of a city?" I found it difficult to imagine people raising tents and staying there for a vacation. Streetcars, cars, and trucks drove along the parks constantly; people walked on sidewalks bordering the gardens; and while it was quiet inside the parks, noise surrounded them.

"America is a very different country from Japan." Uncle Hiroshi stood up. "Wait, I'll be right back." He went into the cave. I heard him rummaging around, and in a few minutes, he came back to the ledge, carrying a geography book.

"That's one of my schoolbooks!" Harumi pointed at it. "Why did you bring it?"

"Everyone can always learn a little more," Uncle Hiroshi said. "Here you will have plenty of opportunity."

"What other books did you bring?" Harumi asked.

"Just history and algebra." Uncle Hiroshi smiled, but Harumi couldn't see it because she had her head bent and stared at the ground.

"And books to read for fun," I added. "Harumi, we can learn from them together."

"I'm not really surprised." Harumi looked up. "The thought of no more lessons was too good to be true. Just promise you won't use a switch across my legs when I make a mistake—that's what my last teacher did."

"Nobody will hit you," Uncle Hiroshi said. "And because this is our first full day here, I declare it a vacation day from school—just like American campers."

"I'll take the book back inside," Harumi said.

"First I want to show you something." Uncle Hiroshi opened the book. "Here's a map of the United States. Look at how much land there is."

I had studied geography several years earlier, and what Uncle Hiroshi pointed out brought back memories of lessons I had learned. Comparing the United States with Japan showed how much larger it was than our country. *How could we possibly prevail against it?*

"Look here and here." Uncle Hiroshi pointed to two places— one in the upper middle of the map and the second farther south and west. "These are two of their parks. Each one is bigger than our entire island of Iejima. Many people camp in these parks each year."

"Did you and Aunty Maiko stay in a park when you traveled in America?" Harumi asked.

"No." Uncle Harumi laughed. "But we did cross the country by train. It was nothing like Japan. Sometimes it was open land for as far as we could see." He closed the book and handed it to Harumi to take back inside.

Mama, who had been putting away the leftover food, joined us on the ledge. "Let's go to the farm for today's water. If each of us fills two buckets every day, we should always have enough for washing and cooking." Our new home did not appear to diminish Mama's energy. Once she had the family shrine in place, she was even cheerful, here on the bluff.

The five of us walked up the path that led to the top of the cliff. Mama was in front, and every once in a while she stopped to point something out to us. At one place, where the trail turned sharply to the left, she told us to look back. We couldn't see our cave, or even the ledge. Thick shrubs and vines blocked them from our view. However, we could look down at the sea where bright turquoise water close to the shore blended into a brilliant blue farther out.

"Remember, Hiroshi, when we were young, how much we found at the shore?"

Mama swept her arm in a gesture that encompassed the expanse of water below. "Instead of looking only to the land for our food, we also have the cove and the beach."

"We had food from the sea back home." I thought of all the fish Gorou brought us, and the dried seaweed we bought at Uncle Hiroshi's market.

"This won't be the same," Uncle Hiroshi said. "Now that we aren't farming, we'll have the time to gather food along the shore. The beaches here are different from Iwa Cove. We'll find much more."

When we reached the end of the path and emerged onto the field that had been part of the farm, Mama told us to put our buckets down. "Before we pump water, let's look around." She turned to the right where the field ended next to a grove of trees, dense with bushes and vines.

"Look, there's a papaya tree." Mama pointed beyond a clump of vines. "In June we should be able to pick the fruit."

"If the fruit bats don't eat them first," Uncle Hiroshi said.

"What bats?" Harumi asked. "I didn't see any bats."

"You've seen them before," I said. "Remember, you called them night ravens."

"Are they around here?" Harumi shivered. "They're frightening."

155

"Have I seen them?" Aunty Maiko asked.

"I don't think so," Uncle Hiroshi said. "If you had, you wouldn't forget them. They're quite large—three feet across."

"Flying foxes," Mama said. "They have faces like dogs and only come out at night. All they eat is fruit. No reason to be frightened."

We walked along the edge of the field while Mama identified more plants she remembered from her childhood on Okinawa. "This is a begonia." She indicated a short plant with dark-green leaves. "We can eat the leaves. Look over there." Mama pointed to a tall grayish-blue plant. "That's a shell ginger. We can use it several ways— wrapping rice, making tea. It's good for our health."

"What's that strange tree?" Harumi pointed to a tall tree that appeared to stand on its roots. "It looks kind of like a mangrove, only different."

"A banyan." Mama pulled Harumi's arm down. "It's bad luck to point at banyans."

"Why?" I asked.

"It's a sacred tree. Hiroshi, do you remember when we played under the roots?"

"I remember being scolded for it." Hiroshi laughed and shook his head. "Our mother said we angered the spirits living under the tree."

"It isn't wise to tempt spirits," Mama said. "You never know how they will avenge their anger."

"*Yare*, we must be careful not to awaken any demons," Aunty Maiko said. "We are not in a good position to face any more bad fortune."

"There's another papaya tree, and a *hirami* lemon." Mama pointed to the left of the banyan. "And a mango, and in front of it— some *bogor* pineapples. This must have been an orchard at one time. If it still bears fruit, we shall have plenty. In fact, we'll eat as well as the emperor."

At the farm, we inspected the buildings more closely than we had earlier. Most of them were collapsed ruins. While the walls of the house still stood, the roof had fallen in with timbers and shingles lying in a mangled heap on the floor. The outhouse was no longer standing; it was a gaping hole surrounded by rotten boards. Luckily, just as it had the day before, after a few squeaky protests from its rusted handle, the pump spewed forth clean, freshwater.

"Girls, I don't want you to go inside any of the farm buildings, and you shouldn't wander in the bushes when it gets dark," Mama said as we headed back to the ledge with our filled buckets.

"I won't be around here after dark. I don't want to see a giant bat." Harumi shook her head for emphasis.

At first I thought Mama was going to warn us about evil spirits, but she had something different in mind.

"A bat won't hurt you, but we must be careful to avoid antagonizing a *habu*. There are more on Okinawa than we have on Iejima."

"I don't ever want to get close to one of those snakes," Harumi said. "I think I know what they look like—they're brown, are they?"

"Some are," Mama said. "There are several different kinds. They're all poisonous. It will be a good idea to stay away from any snake you find. Don't take chances."

I had never had an encounter with a habu. On our island, they were mostly found on Mount Tacchu, where trails up the hill were bordered with thick growth. Even though they were rare on lower ground, where it was more open, we did keep a lookout for them, especially at night, when they became active.

After I saw what plants we could harvest on the abandoned farm, I returned to the cave feeling more optimistic than I had for a long time. Along with the others, I poured my buckets of water into the large barrel we brought from home. A wooden lid covered the cask to protect its contents.

The next day, we were just about to leave the ledge when Gorou appeared. He had walked down the path from the old farm. Two days earlier, when I discovered that he didn't plan to stay with us, I felt both sad and relieved. I was unhappy because I missed him and hoped to regain the closeness we shared during the fall. On the other hand, his absence removed some of discomfort I experienced at his coolness toward me.

"Gorou—you're here!" Harumi said. "Mama and Uncle Hiroshi are taking us down to the beach. We're going to look for *wakame*.

157

Mama says she can use the seaweed to make soup. Will you come with us?"

"Sure." Gorou smiled at my sister's invitation. "But first I want to check on my boat." He looked at Mama, who carried a bucket, and Uncle Hiroshi holding two shovels. "Is there anything I can carry for you?"

"Aunty Maiko has a basket with our lunch in it—could you bring it?" I asked.

"Yes—on one condition," Gorou said. "You walk with me."

And so it was decided. We all went down the path, and when we reached the inlet, while the others veered to the right—toward the beach—Gorou and I turned to the left. Walking past the small landing where we had gotten out of the boat two days before, the path became narrower and muddier.

"Where did you leave your boat?" I asked.

"Behind those mangroves." Gorou pointed to a clump of trees growing out of the mud flats. "Wait here—I'll be right back."

From where I stood, I watched as Gorou slogged through the ooze and reeds to his boat. He checked the ropes, retied one, and grabbed a long-handled fishing net from inside the boat before he rejoined me.

"Let's sit down," he said. "I want to scrape the mud off." He sat on a fallen log and used a short stick to clean his shoes.

"So, how is the place you're staying?" I asked.

"It's fine." Gorou smiled. "I'm at a house just outside Nakijin village. Do you know where that is?"

"No."

"It's not very far from here—about two miles. It's where I've been staying the last three months."

"I didn't know." *Who is he staying with?* I felt a twinge of jealousy.

"The Miyagi family—friends of my grandmother—let me stay with them after I left Iejima. They knew I needed to avoid being noticed by the army after my friend was arrested."

"Oh." The tightness in my chest began to melt as soon as I heard him say "friends of my grandmother."

"I couldn't say anything while we were still on Iejima. It was too dangerous. If the army caught me, it could jeopardize the Miyagis as well as me. And I didn't want to give you the burden of my secret either."

"I understand."

"I'm glad. It was difficult—keeping silent."

When he said the word *secret*, I remembered Gorou telling me that someday he would tell me all his secrets. Maybe I could learn one of them now. "Do you have four brothers?" I asked.

"I don't know, why?"

"Your name—it means 'fifth son.'"

"I might have brothers, but I don't know if I have a family."

"Why not?"

"I was raised by a woman I called Grandmother, but I don't think she was my real grandmother. My mother left me with her when I was a baby. All I know is my name."

"Is that all she told you? Did she say anything about your mother?" I thought about our family and how Mama kept the memory of our ancestors alive and how much the past was part of us. *How different for Gorou—he has no ties.*

"She said my mother was not from Iejima. She might have known more, but she died without telling me."

"I'm so sorry. Was it hard for you?"

"After Grandmother died, the nuns took me in, and when your uncle returned to Iejima, he gave me a job. Then I became a fisherman. Mostly, I consider myself fortunate. I've always received help from good people. Does it bother you that I have no family?"

"Yes—but only because it makes me sad for you. I know people think less of those who have no family standing, but they make superficial judgments."

"I'm glad you feel that way." Gorou smiled and stood up. "Come on, we better join the others on the beach before they fear we sank in a mud pit." He handed me the net and picked up the basket of food. "Harumi will think eating a good lunch is much better than picking seaweed off rocks."

"True. But for her, she likes any activity that isn't algebra." Laughing, we emerged from the shadows of the inlet and joined my family on the beach.

Chapter 20

Portal guardians—
one welcomes and one protects.
Both provide comfort.
　　　　　　　—Atsuko Oshiro

We stayed on the beach for over an hour, wading in the shallows and exploring tide pools. The cool water lapped against our legs, creating a contrast to the late morning's heat. When Aunty Maiko walked up to where we left the lunch basket and started to set out the food, we collected the *wakame* Mama pointed out to us. After we finished filling the bucket, we joined Aunty Maiko, and sat around the rock that served as a makeshift table. Done eating, we returned to the cave, where we rinsed the seaweed in fresh water and spread it on clean sheets to dry in the sun. It was a warm afternoon; everyone relaxed and a comfortable quiet settled on us.

"Gorou, why is your fishing net up here?" Harumi broke the silence.

"I saw palm trees on my way this morning," Gorou said. "Maybe we can find a coconut crab."

"There might be coconut crabs," Uncle Hiroshi said. "But you can't catch them with a net."

"I've never gone after them before," Gorou said. "I thought it would be like capturing them in the water."

"What's a coconut crab?" Aunty Maiko asked.

"Huge crabs that climb trees," Mama said. "Hiroshi and I used to trap them when we were young."

"More accurately, Arisu and I helped our papa," Uncle Hiroshi said. "It's too dangerous for children to try catching coconut crabs without an adult."

"Why are they dangerous?" Harumi asked. "I played with crabs on the beach today. Every time I lifted a rock, they scrambled away to a new hiding place."

"These are different," Uncle Hiroshi said. "For one thing they are much larger." He held his hands several feet apart. "Their legs can by very long, and sharp. Their claws can snap off the finger of a grown man."

"Then I don't think I want one." Harumi wrinkled her nose.

"Ah, but they are delicious," Mama said. "Cooked in boiling water and eaten with rice and vegetables, they make a wonderful dinner."

"This might be the perfect day for us to hunt a coconut crab," Uncle Hiroshi said. "I'll be right back." He went into the cave, and we heard him rustling through a crate. A few minutes later, he emerged, carrying one of the knives we used for cutting tobacco. "I figured this would come in handy."

"What will you do with the knife?" Aunty Maiko asked.

"Prepare the bait," Uncle Hiroshi said. "Gorou, if you take us to the palm trees you saw, we can set a trap. Late afternoon is the best time to catch a coconut crab."

"Can I go?" Harumi asked.

"We can all go," Aunty Maiko said. "This will be another adventure for us."

"While you are on your adventure, take some buckets with you," Mama said. "You can fill them with water to bring back."

"Aren't you coming, Arisu?" Aunty Maiko asked.

"I'll stay here," Mama said. "I can prepare the fire pit so it's ready when you come back. I also want to finish settling our belongings in our new home. The shrine is set up, but I still need to find places for the *shisa*."

I didn't know Mama brought the two lion-dogs that guarded our home on Iejima, but I wasn't surprised. The brass figures had stood on either side of the front entrance for as long as I could remember. When I was very young, Mama told me the male had his mouth closed to protect the house from evil, and the female had her mouth open to share goodness. I wasn't as superstitious as Mama, but those two figures always gave me a feeling of safety. I was glad we had them with us, but I wondered—what would happen to our home, without their protectors?

"Gorou, how far to the palm trees?" Harumi asked as we reached the top of the cliff.

"The trees are a short way past the old farmhouse, to the left." Gorou pointed in the opposite direction we went the day before when we were with Mama.

"Let's leave the buckets here, by the pump," Uncle Hiroshi said. "We can come back and fill them while we wait for our trap to work."

Reaching the palm trees was not easy. No path was visible, and if there had ever been one, it was overgrown. Uncle Hiroshi used his tobacco knife to cut our way to where two palm trees grew.

"Will we find the crabs here?" I asked. "Mama said they crawled on trees."

"Probably not," Uncle Hiroshi said. "But they should be around here—hiding." He pointed to a place about five feet to the left where vines partially covered jagged rocks with deep crevices. "Their day-time homes are in places like this."

"What do we do now? To catch them?" Harumi asked.

"We look around for a coconut or two," Uncle Hiroshi said. "It doesn't matter what condition."

We spread out and wandered around, searching the ground for fallen coconuts. We could have picked one from a tree, but nobody in our group was able to climb to the top where clusters of coconuts hung. Foraging was made difficult by the thick foliage we had to push aside and the vines that seemed to reach out and grab our legs as we walked along. I picked up a small branch to use when I needed to push aside a bush or vine. Remembering Mama's warning, I didn't want to arouse an angry snake. When she saw me with the branch, Harumi did the same. I don't know how she felt, but I would be glad to be back in the open.

"Will this work?" Gorou held up an egg-shaped object covered with what looked like light-brown hair.

"How about this?" Aunty Maiko bent over and grabbed another hairy egg.

"They'll both work," Uncle Hiroshi said. "But this one"—he pointed to the one Aunty Maiko held—"we'll take back with us—it's in good shape—and we can eat it. This one"—he indicated Gorou's coconut—"has started to rot and won't be good eating, but it'll be perfect to attract the attention of Mr. Coconut Crab."

While we watched, Uncle Hiroshi used his knife to cut slices into the coconut and hollowed out part of its insides. He let the milk drip all around the opening. Then he stripped two strands of the covering but didn't remove them. Using the strands as ties, he secured the opened coconut in a wedge between the base of a tree and a rock.

"There, Mr. Crab will smell all that good milk and come to feast," Uncle Hiroshi said. "While we're waiting, we can go fill our buckets. By the time we come back, I imagine we will have something besides water to take back to the cave."

"What if he runs away before we come back?" Harumi asked.

"He won't," Uncle Hiroshi said. "When he starts eating, nothing will stop him, and it'll take a long time before he's done."

Uncle Hiroshi was right. Taking our time, we filled all but one bucket, and carried them to where the path back to the cave began. The remaining bucket went with us back to the trees. Sure enough, the coconut Uncle Hiroshi made into a trap had a visitor. It was the biggest animal with a shell I had ever seen. Its head was buried in the opening of the coconut, held in that position by long, pointed legs. The end of the crab didn't have a stiff shell like the one covering its back; the tail was curled under its abdomen. When we approached the crab, its antennae twitched in all directions, and it waved two large claws in a menacing manner.

"Oh my goodness, he doesn't look very friendly." Aunty Maiko stood a safe distance away.

"No, he isn't," Uncle Hiroshi said. "And we are about to make him even more unhappy. Gorou, you can help me." Uncle Hiroshi cut the strands holding the coconut in the wedge of tree and rock.

Then he grabbed the crab behind its claws and picked it up. While Uncle Hiroshi held the crab, the crab continued to grasp the coconut.

"We need to remove the coconut from its grip," Uncle Hiroshi said. "Grab the coconut where the crab can't reach you, and pull."

Gorou tugged on the coconut; the crab waved his claws and twitched his body, but didn't release its hold. "I can't believe how strong it is," Gorou said. "It's really hanging on."

"Maiko, find a stick," Uncle Hiroshi said. "Give it to Gorou."

She found a small branch and picked it up.

"No, that's not strong enough," Uncle Hiroshi said. "It needs to be bigger."

After looking for a few more minutes, all while the two men struggled with the crab, Aunty Maiko found a sturdier branch.

"That should work," Uncle Hiroshi said. "Gorou, shove the branch between the crab and the coconut, we should be able to pry it loose that way."

Uncle Hiroshi's plan worked, and in a short time, the crab was separated from the coconut. Uncle Hiroshi held the creature away from him as it waved its legs and claws in an attempt to defend itself. With its legs spread out, I could see that Uncle Hiroshi had not exaggerated when he showed us how large a coconut crab could be. This one was more than two feet across.

"Gorou, there's a section of heavy cord in the bucket," Uncle Hiroshi said. "We need to wrap the claws and legs so the crab can't get away, or hurt us."

Gorou tied the claws first, then with Uncle Hiroshi directing him, wrapped the cord around and around, pinning the legs to the crab's body.

"Now it's ready to travel back with us." Uncle Hiroshi set the bound crab in the bucket. "We've had a successful adventure—not only a coconut crab, but also a coconut. Arisu should be pleased."

"I didn't do any of the work, but I feel as though I did." Harumi wiped her sweaty face with her sleeve.

"It's very humid, here among the trees," Aunty Maiko said. "It'll be good to be back along the cliff—there should be a breeze."

"Away from angry coconut crabs and poisonous snakes too." I'd be glad return to the open.

Even though it was the lightest, Uncle Hiroshi carried the bucket with the crab. No one else wanted to. The thought of the creature somehow escaping from its bonds and crawling out of the bucket made me nervous. It must be a very angry crab, and I didn't want to be in its path.

When we reached the cave, I saw Mama had been busy while we were gone. Not only was the fire pit set up, Mama started a fire and put a grill over the glowing coals. Off to the side she had stacked a pile of driftwood. Mama must have made several trips to the beach to gather such a supply of wood. I glanced toward the cave and noticed the two lion-dogs perched on either side of the opening. Mama had somehow fashioned niches for them to stand guard over us, and just as they stood at home, the male was on the left and the female on the right.

"You caught quite a crab." Mama looked into the bucket. "The fire is going strong. I'll put a pot of water to boil and start the rice. We should have a fine dinner."

"Wait," Uncle Hiroshi said. "We brought a coconut back."

"Oh, I can make coconut rice," Mama said. "I haven't had that in a long time."

Uncle Hiroshi opened the coconut so Mama could use its milk in cooking the rice. While the rice steamed, the water in the large pot started to bubble, and Uncle Hiroshi added the crab to it. However, I experienced a twinge when Uncle Hiroshi dropped the crab into the boiling water. While I looked forward to eating it, I also felt sorry for an animal that had fought so hard was about to die a painful death.

"Don't feel too sad." Aunty Maiko must have seen my expression because she reached over and squeezed my arm. "I don't think the poor creature suffered too much."

"I know we have to eat them, but I'm always sorry for the animals we kill." I spoke quietly, so only Aunty Maiko heard me. I didn't want to spoil everyone else's enjoyment.

Along with the coconut rice and the crab, Mama opened a jar of pickled cucumbers for our meal. I ate the crab, savoring its sweet meat, all proving me to be somewhat of a hypocrite.

Shortly after dinner, Gorou stood up to leave. "I want to be back with the Miyagis before it's entirely dark."

"When will you visit again?" Harumi looked up from where she played with Miss Singer, a happy cat enjoying some well-cooked crab.

"I don't know," Gorou said. "The Miyagis are old and need my help. I can't just leave them to fend for themselves. I'll return as soon as I can."

"Before you leave, let me give you something to take with you," Mama said. She put leftover rice, crab, and vegetables in a bamboo container and covered it. "Here, take this to the Miyagis. Ask them if they can be so kind and take this food as a favor to us."

Gorou took the food and gave Mama a short bow. "I'm sure they will do such a favor with gratitude." Then he turned and bowed to the rest of us.

"Wait, I'll walk with you to the path." I stood up, feeling a little self-conscious as I sensed everyone's eyes on me until Harumi stood up also.

"May I walk with you too?" she asked.

"Harumi, I need to talk to you about your lessons," Uncle Hiroshi said.

"Not lessons…" Harumi's voice trailed off.

In the discussion that followed, everyone's attention was diverted from me to my disconsolate little sister.

"You understand why I need to help the Miyagis, don't you?" Gorou asked when we reached the path leading up the cliff, just out of everyone's sight.

"Yes." I knew Gorou wouldn't be the person I cared for if he turned his back on someone in need.

"But I will be back," he said. "Soon."

"I know."

"This war can't last forever." He hesitated. "One day we will be able to think about ourselves—our lives."

I looked up at him. In his eyes I saw the thoughts that he didn't speak—his feelings for me and his hopes for the future.

"You do what you need to. Take care." I touched his arm.

"I will." He gave my hand a squeeze and turned to go. He walked several yards and looked back where I stood watching him leave. With a final wave, he went around a corner and disappeared.

Back on the ledge, Uncle Hiroshi continued talking to Harumi about her lessons. "Education is important."

"I know." Harumi's voice was noticeably unenthusiastic.

"Now, you were supposed to have one vacation day, and somehow that became two," Uncle Hiroshi said. "Tomorrow we will begin—definitely."

"I think we've talked enough about lessons." Aunty Maiko, who had been cleaning up after dinner, came back to the fire. "How about tea?" She filled the iron teakettle and set it over the glowing coals.

"Tell me again how you caught the crab," Mama said when we were drinking our tea.

We all took turns telling her how we found the coconuts, how Uncle Hiroshi set the trap, and what happened when the crab came. It grew darker, and Mama threw more wood on the fire. For a long time after we finished our story, we silently watched the flames until they slowly died down, leaving only embers.

"It's late." Uncle Hiroshi yawned. "If you light a lantern to take inside, I'll douse the fire."

It only took a few minutes for us to wash our hands and faces by the lantern's light, then enter the cave and find our futons. For a little while I could hear soft noises as everyone settled into their quilted mattresses, then it was just soft breathing.

I stayed awake, thinking over the events of the day—thinking about Gorou and what I learned about his life. For years, I only knew him as the young man who worked for my uncle. While I was aware he had no family, I didn't know his mother abandoned him as an infant. I felt like crying for the lost little boy he must have been. Maybe that's why he was always so willing to help others. I thought of all the times he came to help my family—even using his precious fuel to bring us to safety. A frightening thought suddenly occurred to me—safety! Gorou's safety. How much had he risked by coming back to Iejima to help us move? If he'd been stopped by the military, he might have been executed, just as his friend had been. However, during the entire time he helped us pack our belongings and brought us to Okinawa, he never indicated it was tedious, let alone extremely dangerous. I thought about what he said when he left earlier that night—about us and our future. A feeling of joy surged through me. We must be hopeful, and look to the end of the war, and pray it will be over soon.

For the next few weeks, my optimism prevailed. Our days passed pleasantly on the ledge. It was springtime, the weather became warmer, and we had plenty to eat. Then it all came crashing down— the horrors of war erupted all around us with terrifying destruction. The struggle to survive became worse than anything I could imagine.

Chapter 21

Sister Harumi,
impulsive, like spring weather,
just as beautiful.
—Atsuko Oshiro

It wasn't unusual to see airplanes flying overhead; I had seen them
frequently ever since the war started. However, as the end of March
approached, their presence increased dramatically. Months before,
when the fighting was in the Philippine Sea and Leyte Gulf, planes
flew overhead at great altitude—small black birds heading south to
certain death. The planes we saw over Okinawa were much lower.
The flag of Japan with the rising sun was easily visible under the
wings, as were the numbers painted on the sides. Occasionally I
caught glimpses of the pilots' faces, grim with the knowledge they
flew to their own immolation.

Uncle Hiroshi brought our radio when we left our farm, but
every time we attempted to listen, there was no reception. The only
information we had was that Japan's military forces were now concentrated in the southern part of Okinawa—a piece of news Gorou
passed on to us. Other than that, he could tell us very little. After
his army friend had been executed and Gorou began to avoid contact with the military, his channel of information evaporated. It was
unsettling to see a steady stream of military planes flying over every
day and imagine they were gathering for a major confrontation. Our
ignorance increased the dread and fear overtaking our lives.

As ominous as the constant flight of planes overhead became,
we didn't let the threat of danger overwhelm us. We planned a cele-

bration for Harumi's birthday. She turned fourteen on the last day of March, and we wanted to make the day special for her.

When I thought of my fourteenth birthday, I felt sorry for Harumi and her experiences. My birthday was spent with friends at school, a small celebration at lunch, and a dinner of my favorite food. Sayuri spent the night, and we giggled and acted as silly as we wanted. Harumi's life was a stark contrast to that. In less than a year, we lost Mr. Brave, worked harder than ever, gave away most of our food, and were evicted from the only home we'd ever known. To add to her hardships, Harumi didn't have the companionship of people her own age. Remembering how many friends she once had, I realized how difficult it must have been. In some small way, I wanted to make it up to her.

The morning of Harumi's birthday started auspiciously. The day before had been warm, but rainy; however, on her birthday, the sun shone and the air felt fresh. Uncle Hiroshi gave Harumi her first gift.

"Today you have no lessons," he said.

"Thank you! Oh, thank you!" Harumi's smile added to her words of gratitude.

"It's a vacation day for Atsuko and me, also." Uncle Hiroshi's smile mirrored my sister's. "We can all be fourteen today."

As a happy coincidence, the tide that morning was lower than usual, and part of the coral reef bordering the shore lay exposed. The five of us walked down the path to the beach with buckets, knives, and trowels to gather gifts from the sea. Once we rounded the curve that separated the inlet from the open shore, we could walk out along the crusty reef dotted with tide pools. Because the terrain was irregular, some of the pools were small and shallow, while others were deep enough to swim in.

"Atsuko, come here." Harumi crouched along the edge of one of the larger pools. "Look." She pointed to the small bright-blue fish darting around the coral. "Do you know what those are called?"

"Let's ask Mama," I said.

Mama came over when Harumi gestured to her. "Those are blue damselfish. This is a big pool; you might be able to see a parrotfish. Keep looking—they blend in with the rocks."

Harumi leaned over closer and held herself still, staring into the water. "Oh!" She jumped back, startled. "There." She pointed. "I thought it was a rock, but it moved. Can you see it?"

I looked down and saw a striped fish, larger than the damselfish, poking its head between two brown rocks. It opened its mouth and revealed protruding teeth. "Does it bite?" I asked.

"Just smaller fish," Mama said. "I think it's very shy. Keep looking—you might see an octopus." She stood up and started to walk away. "Call me if you do—they are delicious."

We didn't find an octopus, but the longer we searched the tide pool, the more creatures we saw. Tiny starfish with delicate arms, brown crabs walking sideways and waving their claws, snails and limpets that blended in with the rocks. It reminded me of the time I visited the aquarium in Kyoto with Papa.

"Girls! Come here!" Mama was next to a pool farther down the beach. "I'm going to show you how to catch a sea cucumber."

When she indicated the reddish-brown creature, I didn't think it would be too difficult to scoop it into a bucket, and I grabbed a trowel.

"Wait," Mama said. "Perhaps we can make our job easier." She took the trowel from me and prodded the animal having the shape of a large cucumber, with its overgrown wormlike body and soft spines. At first, nothing happened. "Hmm." Mama prodded again, harder. Then the strangest thing—the sea cucumber arched as though to move, but while it did that, the creature began to drop part of itself on the ground—its stomach.

"Oh! What's it doing?" Its action repulsed me.

"Ah, just what I wanted it to do," Mama said. "Now we don't have to clean it. It's a trick sea cucumbers use when they want to escape an enemy. If we were starfish, we'd leave it alone after it spit out its stomach." She scooped the now limp sea cucumber into a bucket. "Now let's see if we can find a few clams."

We walked past several shallow tide pools until Mama stopped at one. "This appears to be a good place to find clams." She crouched and started to dig in the sand at the bottom of the pool. The top layer was light brown, but a few inches underneath the sand became a dark, almost black color. "Here's what we want." Mama flipped a clump of dark sand toward me. "Rinse it off, there's an *ubagai* in it."

I dipped the black gob in the pool, and the sand melted off, leaving the smooth, closed shell of a clam. I placed it in one of the buckets in time to catch the next clam Mama sent my direction. Meanwhile, Harumi found the large half shell of a long dead clam and used it as a trowel and joined in the digging. For the next few minutes, we were busy, with Mama and Harumi digging and me putting the rinsed clams into a bucket.

"We have enough." Mama stopped us when the bucket was nearly half full. "With the sea cucumber, I can make a stew tonight." She took the bucket and rinsed it several more times, leaving the clams covered with a few inches of water. "Let's see what Hiroshi and Maiko have found."

My aunt and uncle were bent over a green mass clinging to the exposed rocks. Aunty Maiko was helping Uncle Hiroshi cut seaweed to put in a bucket. "Hiroshi has been teaching me how to harvest seaweed—look." She held up the bucket. "He calls this *umi budo*." Aunty Maiko pointed to what appeared to be strings of green pearls.

"Yes, sea grapes," Mama said. "A wonderful addition to rice dishes. And I see you have a collection of *asa*. We can use the sea lettuce to make soup. The low tide has been very generous today—we should have an excellent feast tonight."

With full buckets, we gathered our tools and left the reef. As we crossed the beach to the path, I became aware, once again, of the planes overhead. The sound of droning engines added to the threat of their presence.

"Sometimes, I can almost forget how they constantly fly across our lives." Aunty Maiko looked up and shuddered. "And then, when I can't ignore them, the planes become most unwelcome guests."

"Let's try to go back to ignoring them," Mama said. "We have a special celebration today."

Even with our limited resources, we did give Harumi a wonderful birthday. Aunty Maiko suggested, since we brought our finest clothes to the cave, we dress for dinner.

"This is an important day for Harumi," she said. "I think we should make an effort to look our best for the occasion."

She and Mama put on their embroidered kimonos, while I wore the jacket Aunty Maiko made for my birthday in September, and Uncle Hiroshi was dressed in his good suit. Harumi mentioned that her kimono was tight on her, but she looked well-dressed. Altogether, we made an elegant appearance.

After a dinner made with our bounty from the coral reef, we gave my sister the gifts we somehow managed to put together. I had found an old photograph of Harumi, aged eight, sitting on Mr. Brave with Papa standing next to her. Uncle Hiroshi made a frame for the picture so Harumi could display it.

"Mr. Brave! And Papa!" Harumi hugged the photograph to her chest. "Thank you, Atsuko and Uncle Hiroshi. I'll keep this forever. Thank you!"

Aunty Maiko's present was next. She had made a silk jacket; it was similar to the one she gave me a few months earlier. It was embroidered in the vibrant colors and symbols that represented the Ryukyu Islands.

"It's beautiful!" Harumi removed the tissue wrapping and held the jacket up. She stood to put it on and turned around so we could admire it. "I love it! It's the most beautiful thing I've ever owned." She hugged Aunty Maiko.

Mama gave her gift last. She handed Harumi a small wooden box. Harumi's eyes widened before she even opened it. The box was familiar: it had sat on Mama's dressing table for as long as I could remember. Harumi removed the lid, holding her breath, then exhaled while she slowly lifted a circlet of gold.

"Your bracelet—you're giving me your bracelet?" She fingered the gold as though she couldn't believe it was real.

"My mother gave it to me when I was your age," Mama said. "It's time I passed it on to you. You're a young lady now."

Harumi didn't say anything; she just looked at us, her eyes filled with tears. "This is the best birthday ever. I'll never forget this day, as long as I live." She hugged each of us in turn—even Uncle Hiroshi, who paused a moment, then hugged her back. Harumi laughed, pulled back, and gave a short bow. "I know, I should act proper and respectful."

"So should I." Uncle Hiroshi bowed in return. "Look." He pointed to the eastern sky. A full moon crested over the hill. "Perhaps that is a sign of good fortune."

"Well, today was filled with good fortune." Harumi sat quietly and smiled down at the photograph and the box with the bracelet.

The night was so mild we remained outside for a long time; Uncle Hiroshi started to yawn, and soon the rest of us joined him.

"It's time we went inside," Aunty Maiko said. "As pleasant as today has been, I'm looking forward to a good night's sleep."

Before lying down, I knelt at my desk and lifted the lid. "Harumi, this is where I keep the opal ring Mama gave me for my fourteenth birthday. Would you like to keep your bracelet in here also?"

"Yes. Thank you, Atsuko. Your desk is the perfect place to keep my bracelet safe."

Afterward, as I lay on my futon, I thought, Harumi was right—this was a wonderful day. If the rest of our time here was like this, our lives weren't going to be unbearable.

The very next day, the nightmare began. We were on top of the cliff, heading back to the cave with buckets we filled at the old farm, when the sky became dark with a mass of planes flying overhead. The planes didn't have Japanese flags painted on the wings. They wore the stars and stripes of the United States. They swooped over us—aircraft on a deadly mission.

"We need to get back to the cave! Hurry!" Mama's voice was urgent and frightened. "We should be safe in the cave. The Americans have no reason to attack us there."

Staying close to the cliff, we made our way back to the ledge. The others went into the cave while Uncle Hiroshi and I covered the table, the water barrel, and fire pit with bushes. "From the air, they shouldn't be able to tell anyone is here," Uncle Hiroshi said.

"What about Gorou's boat?" I asked.

"He has it deep in the inlet," Uncle Hiroshi said. "Hopefully, the canopy of the mangrove trees will keep it hidden. Now let's get into the cave."

For the next three days, we huddled in the dark cave and listened to the nearly constant sound of planes, occasionally punctuated by the distant explosion of bombs. Once again, it was the unknown that intensified our fear. Whenever there was a lull, we would timidly emerge from the cave—to get water or use the toilet, but we never left the ledge. For short intervals, we lit a lantern, but since we didn't want to deplete our supply of oil, it wasn't kept burning very long.

On the fourth day, I woke to quiet—no planes and no bombs. The quiet lasted long enough to create the impression it was all over. We sat on the ledge, and Uncle Hiroshi built a fire. For the first time since Harumi's birthday, it appeared as though we would have a normal day. Mama had just poured tea, when a slight noise above startled us. A few seconds later, Gorou appeared—walking down the path from the cliff. He carried a rolled bundle held together with straps on his back.

"Gorou—surprised to see you!"

"You're here!"

"What's going on?"

"What has happened?"

"Why have you come?"

We all spoke at once, but Gorou didn't say anything at first. He took a deep breath before starting to talk.

"I need your help. I didn't have any other place to go."

"What about the Miyagis?" Mama asked. "Are they all right?"

"I don't know," Gorou said. "They're gone. They left five days ago. Yesterday a bomb destroyed their house. I thought, if I came here, I could sleep in my boat."

"Nonsense," Mama said. "You'll stay here, with us. In our cave you'll be safer than sleeping in the open. Now tell us what you know about the bombing."

"I don't know very much," Gorou said. "But the war has come to Okinawa."

Gorou's words stayed with me, echoing over and over in my mind. Later that day, I took out paper and pen, attempting to capture my feelings.

> Pity homeless birds,
> Cowering in the darkness,
> Their hopes begin to fade.
> *(Atsuko Oshiro)*

Chapter 22

What is the color of fear? Maybe the long hours we spent in darkness influenced me to begin visualizing emotions in different shades. Japanese culture had always given significance to colors; the meanings I knew were favorable, such as yellow for courage and beauty, or green for eternal life and youthfulness. Such positive feelings didn't fit the life I experienced trapped in a world of unknown danger. Where black symbolized mystery and fascination, I knew the blackness surrounding us for the hours we huddled in the cave was the color of numbing boredom. Fear? I couldn't think of a color harsh enough; maybe it was sudden flashes of harsh light, bursts that rushed toward us—no color—just a throbbing brightness—images coexisting with the painful cramps that clenched my muscles whenever the noise intensified.

The month of April crept by, our days accompanied by the steady drone of airplanes overhead, occasionally punctuated by the sound of bombs exploding. In the midst of all this horror, we strived to maintain a routine. During times of quiet, we'd leave the safety of the cave and go to the shore for quick food searches, or up on the cliff for water and edible plants. On our hurried trips, we stayed as close to cover as possible, and when we were in the open, we didn't linger. Even though we heard the explosion of bombs, it appeared as though our remote part of Okinawa wasn't a target and no one was looking to destroy our cliff. Uncle Hiroshi said he believed no one was searching for us specifically; if we didn't call attention to ourselves, we'd be left alone. His words gave me a sliver of hope.

The first day Gorou was with us, he described what happened to the Miyagis and their house. Soon after the skies filled with planes, a small group of Japanese soldiers came to the village of Nakijin and urged the residents to leave. They offered transport to a camp farther south.

"And the Miyagis decided to leave?" Uncle Hiroshi asked.

"Yes," Gorou said. "Mr. Miyagi claimed they were old and useless. He didn't expect me to take care of them anymore. I couldn't talk them out of their decision."

"But the soldiers didn't want to take you?" Aunty Maiko asked.

"I wasn't there while the soldiers were in Nakijin. I returned while the Miyagis were preparing to leave. I made sure the soldiers never saw me."

"What will happen to them now?" Harumi asked.

I saw a look pass between Gorou and Uncle Hiroshi. Neither one said anything, but Uncle Hiroshi mouthed the words *shudan jiketsu*. Even unspoken, the presence of those two evil words had the power to poison the air around us. I felt sick at the thought of the elderly couple becoming part of a mass suicide. I had known about people being encouraged to perform the "honorable act" ever since Uncle Hiroshi told us about it more than a year before. However, I didn't see anything honorable about ending my life, especially since it was just beginning, and I was grateful to Mama and Uncle Hiroshi for not following the directives of the military.

"I don't know what's going to happen," Gorou said. "But a few days after they left, the Americans bombed most of the houses in Nankijin, so it's just as well they had gone."

"Why destroy a small village?" I asked. "It's not as if it's important."

"I don't know that either," Gorou said. "They even damaged part of the castle, and it's already a ruin."

When Gorou joined us in the cave, he apologized for being a burden, but his presence was a welcome addition. As always, he helped us with the challenges we faced, living in somewhat primitive conditions. My feelings about his presence were a mix of gladness and guilt. I could be with him every day, but my happiness was tempered with self-reproach when I thought of the terrible fate the Miyagis faced and the destruction of their home. I also knew I needed to maintain my decorum, since all our actions would be watched over by my observant mother and properly-mannered aunt and uncle.

In the midst of all the horror that had become part of our existence in the cave, not everything in our lives was dreary. Ever since she turned fourteen, Harumi began to change. She still moved quickly, and spoke frankly, but much of her reckless impulsiveness had disappeared, and she became more thoughtful and considerate. Her looks changed also. She had grown taller than I, and while my features, like Mama, were more rounded, Harumi was all angles— from her cheekbones to her elbows that stuck out when she walked. She even abandoned her favorite word—*stupid*—much to Uncle Hiroshi's relief. However, she still balked at her lessons, particularly math, with Uncle Hiroshi.

"What difference does it make how much *tatami* the governor needs to cover his floors?" Harumi threw her pencil down in frustration. "I'm never going to sell it to him, or go to his house." But before Uncle Hiroshi could reply, she paused to take a breath and picked up her pencil. "I'm sorry, can you help me with this problem?" She finished the rest of her math problems without another outburst.

I particularly remember one day when I gave her a history lesson. It was during one of the days we sat in the dark, and I told Harumi something I knew by heart. "Our islands haven't always been a part of Japan. The castle Gorou said has been bombed was built over seven hundred years ago as a fortress for the Sanzan Kingdom. Six hundred years ago, the kingdom joined with the other areas of the Okinawa islands to become the Ryukyu Kingdom."

"That's really a long time ago." Harumi didn't sound very interested.

"Think about it," I said. "It's our heritage. The Ryukyu Kingdom was very powerful. The Chinese would trade with us, but not with Japan. Japan traded with us, but not with China. Our seagoing merchants sailed to faraway ports to buy and sell goods. Our sailors traveled beyond China—they went to Vietnam, Korea, even as far as Siam."

"They did that all those years ago?" Harumi asked. "They must have been brave."

"Yes, they crossed the sea to those distant countries when Europeans still thought the world was flat and they could fall off the edge."

"Oh!" Harumi giggled.

"And consider the goods brought to each country. Japan produced silver, swords, and lacquerware, while China sold medicine, coins, ceramics, and textiles. Other countries traded wood, tin, sugar, ivory, and incense."

"That would be exciting." Harumi's voice reflected her rising interest.

"Think about how it would be when a ship came into port. People gathered at the piers, eager to see what had been delivered. Men bartering for the cargo, excited about the treasures that arrived. And the sailors, relieved to reach land after lengthy, and sometimes dangerous, voyages."

"And those were our ancestors—brave sailors! What happened to the Ryukyu Kingdom?"

"We were taken over by the Japanese shogunate over two hundred years ago, but were still allowed to trade with China. Then about seventy years ago, we became a part of Japan—like the rest of the country."

"But we're not like the rest of Japan."

"No, we're not. Our culture has many elements. We are a combination of all the countries we traded with. We celebrate the lunar New Year, we use colorful symbols, and many of our traditions are not the same as the rest of Japan. The way we live is made up of bits and pieces from many places. We should be proud."

"I am—now." Harumi reached over in the darkness and gave my hand a squeeze. "If history at my school in Ginoza was taught the way you teach, I would have liked it."

"What was wrong with the way you learned?"

"Our teacher was mean, and he didn't like us. All he talked about was how much we should honor the emperor because he took care of his children."

"He didn't like you? He was mean?"

"Yes. He always said things like we 'weren't as valuable as dogs' and weren't 'worth the trouble' it was to teach us."

"You weren't worth the trouble? Are you sure he said that?" I began to understand Harumi's attitude toward school.

"His used the words 'inferior curs,' and sometimes I thought he would have liked to put us in kennels."

"Harumi, I'm sorry." I thought about the lessons I had, and how much I looked forward to school. The nuns could be demanding and strict, but I didn't remember them ever calling us names or treating us as worthless. Poor Harumi.

After what felt like months, one day I woke up to silence. No planes flew overhead, and I heard no bombing. We emerged from the cave, blinking in the bright, unfamiliar light, and planned a short trip for water. It turned out to be an opportunity for Gorou and me to spend time together, just the two of us. We returned before the others—they stayed on top of the cliff to pick fruit. Sitting on the ledge, we enjoyed the sun's warmth as we talked.

At first our conversation was general—I talked about Harumi's lessons, and he said he thought there was more kerosene still at the Miyagis and wanted to go there and bring it back. For a while we sat there in a companionable silence—until Gorou turned and looked into my eyes.

"Atsuko?"

"Yes."

"Does my handicap bother you?"

At first I didn't know what he meant. "Your foot?" I said after a short pause. "I never think of you as having a handicap." Gorou was so strong and capable; I hadn't thought about his limp for a long time. "It doesn't stop you from doing anything. It just seems to be part of you, like your smile."

"I want to tell you about something that happened when I was twelve." He paused, and when he started talking again, he spoke slowly, choosing his words carefully. "Sometimes the other boys said cruel things to me—because I couldn't run as fast as them, and if I tried to keep up, I stumbled. Growing up without a proper family, I

181

usually ignored the things that made me feel different and left out. But one day, Sister Mary Josephine overheard those boys teasing me."

"What did she do?" My heart went out to the young Gorou whose childhood had been so difficult.

"Nothing to the boys, and I was glad. If she had interfered, they would have only increased their taunts. Instead, she waited until no one else was around and spoke to me about the situation."

"Did it help?"

"In a way. She told me everyone has problems, and when we learn to offer up our suffering, the Lord will help us."

That sounded familiar. Nuns were great for telling us to "offer it up for the poor souls" whenever we were unhappy or faced a difficulty. As much as it irritated me, it did cure me of whining about petty problems—at least to the nuns. "Did she say anything else?"

"She said it was unfortunate I was born with a twisted foot, but think about the people in the world who were born with a twisted soul and asked me which one would I pick. Of course I told her I didn't want a twisted soul. Then she told me about a famous American— Thaddeus Stevens—who was a friend of Abraham Lincoln. He worked hard to pass an amendment that made slavery illegal. And he had a clubfoot. She said there have been many important people with the same handicap who went on to achieve greatness."

"What happened after that—with the other boys?"

"I did what I always did. I ignored them. Eventually, they stopped, and not long afterward, I began fishing. While I'm out on the water in my boat, my lame foot doesn't get in the way."

We sat for a few moments in silence. I thought of the young Gorou who learned about coping with a twisted foot and developing a strong character.

"There's something else. You saw me that day, didn't you?" Gorou spoke in a quiet voice.

I knew what day he meant. That terrible day when the soldiers came for Sister Dominica. When they surrounded Gorou in front of the market, sliced his clothes, and made fun of him. The image of what I saw was permanently etched in my brain. "You just stood there. I didn't know anyone could stand so still while being assaulted."

"I was afraid for my safety and realized it was best not to react. Also, I knew some of the soldiers had taken Sister Dominica back inside the school. They were attacking her. If I kept some of the soldiers outside with me, that meant fewer rapes for her to endure."

As I heard his simple words, I was overcome with feeling. His story made me feel humble and care for him all the more. I reached over, took his hand, and sandwiched it between my two. For a while, we sat close together in silence.

The sound of an approaching plane interrupted the silence. When I looked up to the north, I saw the plane wasn't moving in the usual way. It traveled in spurts and pauses, the wings dipped haphazardly, and the engine sputtered. When it was directly overhead, the plane turned into a nosedive. At first I thought it would crash into us, but it missed; passing so close to the ledge, I could have reached out and touched the rising sun painted on the underside of its wing. Then it crashed into the trees growing in the inlet below.

"Gorou!" I jumped up and tugged on Gorou's sleeve, pulling him to his feet. "We have to go see! Maybe the pilot's still alive! The plane—may have crashed into your boat!" My shouted words came out in a rushed jumble. We ran down the path to see what disaster had landed below.

Chapter 23

Not the gentle rain,
But steel falling from the sky,
Men caught in a cage.
                    —Atsuko Oshiro

We hurried to where the fallen plane perched precariously in a mangrove tree. Its nose pointed to the ground, and the wings swayed back and forth, creaking ominously against the branches supporting them. A uniformed arm dangled at an awkward angle out the window of the cockpit, and I heard a feeble voice say, "Help me." Then nothing.

"He's still alive!"

"I think I can reach him." Gorou hoisted himself up the tree and slid along a branch until he could open the door to the cockpit. "He's wedged in here, but I should be able to pull him out." After what seemed like a long time, Gorou managed to extricate the pilot from the plane and perch him on the branch. Grasping him firmly around his chest, Gorou pulled the man back to the tree trunk, hoisted him over his shoulder, and carried him down to the ground.

"He's just a boy!" Looking at the young Japanese pilot as he lay on the grass, I saw he couldn't have been much older than me. In addition to his left arm bending grotesquely outward, a gash went from the crown of his head across his forehead and bled profusely. He was very thin. I removed my light cotton jacket and used it to wipe the blood from his face, then wrapped it as best I could around his injury. "We need to get him back to the cave. Mama will know what to do."

"Fortunately, he's not very heavy." Gorou lifted the man up and draped him across his shoulders. The pilot groaned loudly once and retched, leaving a trail of yellow bile and phlegm trailing down Gorou's back. "I'll try not to jolt him, but we should get him to the cave as quickly as possible."

The walk up the path to the cave was slow; periodically I used the sleeve of my jacket to wipe the blood that continued to drip from the head wound. We reached the ledge and saw the others had returned from their short expedition.

"We were wondering where you two ran off—Oh!" Harumi came up to us and interrupted herself when she noticed Gorou carried someone.

"Here, let me help you." Uncle Hiroshi rushed up and held the pilot's shoulders as Gorou slid out from under him. Carefully, they lowered the man to the ground so he lay on his back.

Just as I thought she would, Mama took command of the situation. "I'll need to clean him up and do something about his arm before we move him into the cave." She knelt beside the unconscious man and carefully unwrapped my jacket from his head. "Maiko, can you bring some towels and an old sheet? Atsuko, build up the fire and heat some water. Harumi, you take care of the food and water we brought back." Mama folded my jacket into sort of a pillow for the pilot's head and carefully felt along his arm to find where it had been broken.

"Hiroshi, I think if we use slats from a crate, we can make a splint for his arm. But first, I must set the bone. I'll need a knife also."

Uncle Hiroshi nodded. "I'll get the boards and a knife. I've never set a broken bone before, you'll have to show me what to do."

"Living on a farm, I've seen many injuries. I haven't had much experience with broken bones, but I should be able to twist his back into its proper place. I want to have the splints and cloth prepared before we begin. It's good he's unconscious."

Aunty Maiko handed Mama a sheet, and she ripped it into strips. She dipped a towel into the water, gently washed the head wound, and wrapped a strip over the gash. Then she took a deep breath before she began on the broken arm. "Hold his shoulders steady. I'm going to cut off his sleeve and then move the bone back in place." Mama directed Uncle Hiroshi and Gorou to either side of the pilot's head. "Maiko, have the splints and bindings ready. If I can put the bone back where it belongs, I don't want it to have a chance of slipping out again."

The entire time Mama worked over the injured man, I hardly breathed. From the tense way the others held themselves, I don't think they were breathing much either. Mama carefully ran her hands over the broken arm to feel where the bone was fractured. Then, holding the arm above the break, she pulled and twisted until the lower section of the arm was rotated back into place. Just as the bone moved into place, the man's eyes flickered opened, he moaned, and fell back into unconsciousness.

"Turn him on his side so I can attach the splint." Mama held the broken arm steady while Uncle Hiroshi and Gorou carefully turned the pilot to his right. "Maiko, help me place a board on either side of his arm, and, Atsuko, wrap the cloth around the splints—make it tight."

I bound the boards and the arm as tightly as I could, but Mama finished the task by pulling the bindings even more taut. She had Uncle Hiroshi and Gorou hold him by the shoulders while she bound the splinted arm to his chest.

"That's the best we can do for now." Mama stood up, moving stiffly. Her face was pale, and beads of sweat covered her forehead. "Oh dear." She staggered a little. "I need to sit down for a bit."

"Arisu, you were marvelous." Aunty Maiko looked at Harumi. "Would you make tea for your mother?"

"The water's hot, I'll make some for everyone." Harumi looked down at the unconscious man. "What about him? His mouth looks very dry."

"We can't give him anything to drink, not while he's like this," Mama said. "It's too dangerous—he could swallow the wrong way and drown. Atsuko, would you moisten a towel and rub it over his lips?"

Harumi busied herself with making a pot of tea and gathering cups while I wiped the pilot's mouth with a wet cloth. Gorou went into the cave to change out of his soiled clothing. When he rejoined us, we began drinking our tea. For a few minutes, no one said anything; we just watched the labored breathing of the injured man.

"Oh my, you have such an admirable skill." Aunty Maiko gave Mama a slight nod. "When did you learn to set broken bones?"

"Today." Mama smiled weakly and sipped her tea. "I didn't know I could do it. Necessity makes a good teacher. The only time I did anything similar to this was when Atsuko was eight years old. She fell while playing on the rocks at Iwa Cove and sprained her ankle."

"Oh! I almost forgot!" Harumi turned to Gorou and me. "We have news. Tell them, Uncle Hiroshi."

"Yes," Uncle Hiroshi said. "We met a family near the old farmhouse. There were three of them—an older man, his wife, and a daughter. They were headed to a new place to live—somewhere safer."

"Where were they going? And why?" I asked.

"They were walking east. The man, Mr. Hano, said friends of theirs had a house in the woods, and he hoped they could live with them. He told us their house in Nakijin had been partly destroyed, but the real reason they left was because Americans now control the north part of Okinawa. They are rounding up the Japanese and taking them to refugee camps."

"Mr. Hano said he wanted to avoid the American devils," Harumi said. "He said he heard the soldiers torture Japanese citizens and rape the women, then they shoot them."

"We don't know for sure that is the way Americans behave, but they are our enemies, and we should be cautious." Uncle Hiroshi's voice deepened with seriousness. "We need to disguise our presence on the ledge and be more careful about where we go and when. Our best plan is to stay out of sight during the day and avoid open places, such as the field near the farmhouse and the beach. Even walking on the path can be dangerous. So far, the only time we've stayed in the cave was when we heard planes. Now we will have to remain inside even more. No one is looking for us, and we don't want to give them a reason to start."

"If we don't want to be noticed, we should try to move the plane," Gorou said. "Its tail is visible above the tree." He turned to Uncle Hiroshi. "Will you come with me? I also want to move my boat. It's directly under one of the wings."

"Before you go, will you carry him into the cave?" Mama pointed to the pilot. "Where we can try to keep him comfortable."

"He can use my futon," Gorou said. "I'll sleep on the ground."

Mama went into the cave and lit the lantern. She unrolled Gorou's futon and laid it out with the head end against the wall. Uncle Hiroshi and Gorou picked the man up, and with Uncle Hiroshi holding his legs and Gorou his shoulders, they moved him into the cave's main room and placed him on the mattress.

Harumi and I went back down to the inlet with Uncle Hiroshi and Gorou, leaving Mama and Aunty Maiko fussing over the injured man. When we reached the plane, I saw that it had tilted to the left and slipped farther down the tree; one of its wings almost touched the boat. The first thing Gorou did was to move his boat away from the plane. He pushed it to the other side of the inlet where it was hidden behind bushes and a fallen tree. He rejoined us in looking at the plane.

"It looks pretty flimsy," Harumi said.

"It's a kamikaze plane," Uncle Hiroshi said. "Built to be destroyed. Look—it has no landing gear."

"You mean?" I asked.

"Yes," Uncle Hiroshi said. "This plane was designed to drop the landing gear when it became airborne. It can take off, but never land—only crash."

I thought about the young man who lay on Gorou's futon, fighting for his life. What were his emotions when he took off in this plane, knowing he flew into his death—a violent and painful demise? He was so young; he should have his life stretching out before him, full of plans and ambitions. Not a horrible finality.

"Most of this plane has a wooden frame, and it's not that solid." Gorou climbed up the tree and began to tug on a wing. "If I can pull this away from the branch, we should be able to make the plane fall some more."

Uncle Hiroshi climbed partway up the trunk and grabbed the tip of the wing while Harumi and I pulled on the wing closest to the ground. After a few minutes, our efforts succeeded; the plane shifted and slipped some more.

"I'm going to climb up higher and push on the tail," Gorou said. "Stay clear, I don't want it hitting anyone." He reached the plane's tail by wrapping his legs around the tree and stretching toward it. The tree swayed every time he moved, and I was certain he would come crashing down at any moment. Luckily, Gorou remained perched; and after he pushed and jerked the plane's tail, it finally gave way. Because one wing hung below the branches and Uncle Hiroshi and Gorou had freed the other, once the tail lost its support, the plane slid from the tree and landed in the water.

Gorou climbed down and looked at the plane slowly sinking into the water. "Once it sinks to the bottom, the mud will swallow it, and no one will know it's there."

I looked up; I tried to imagine what could be seen from overhead. All I saw were the leaf-covered branches of the mangrove trees. *How did we manage to maneuver a plane through the branches with their dense foliage? It looks impossible.* I shrugged, not knowing the answer.

The others had started back up the path, and I hurried to join them.

What followed were long days and longer nights, as we kept ourselves enclosed in the cave. Those days and nights were different from what they had been before the pilot dropped into our lives. Planes weren't flying over constantly. Perhaps because of what Mr. Hano told Uncle Hiroshi—the fighting had shifted to the southern part of Okinawa. Silence surrounded us, accompanied by the dread of the unknown. *Will American soldiers come looking for us? What will happen to us?* But the big question was how could we save the injured man? Most of the time he lay quietly, and Mama wiped his face with a wet cloth. She also changed the bandaging on his head wound, and eventually it began to heal. At times he became restless and mumbled incoherently or groaned loudly.

We kept the lantern lit more than we had earlier. The light made it possible to attend the unconscious man. And we talked. Our voices seemed to calm him, and he would stop thrashing about, jeopardizing the makeshift binding on his arm. Even Miss Singer joined us in soothing the pilot. She would curl up next to his uninjured side and commence purring.

Harumi told folktales—the same ones she learned from Papa years before and had used when she talked to Mr. Brave. I read from my books, tales of Japanese heroes from centuries long past. Aunty Maiko and Mama told us about events from their past, stories we had heard before, and enjoyed hearing again.

"I'll never forget the time we saw Emperor Hirohito," Aunty Maiko said. "It was more than twenty years ago—in London. Such an event couldn't have happened in Japan."

"Why?" Harumi asked, even though she knew the answer.

"The emperor is divine, and no one is allowed to look at him. Most of the time he lives in seclusion with his family at the Imperial Palace."

"That sounds so lonely," I said. "It's almost as if he's a prisoner."

"And it's what makes what we saw in London so extraordinary," Aunty Maiko said. "The British treat their monarchs very differently. People line the streets to catch a glimpse of the royal family. At parades, the king and queen ride in open carriages and wave to their subjects. Hirohito joined the British royalty in public. It was even said that he played golf with a duke."

"It made for problems when he returned to Japan," Uncle Hiroshi said. "He tried to change some the restrictions on his life. He even urged his ministers to form treaties with England and the United States."

"The emperor did manage to go against his advisors when he married the woman he himself had chosen. And he's never taken a concubine," Aunty Maiko said.

"Unfortunately, he has listened to bad advice about war," Uncle Hiroshi said. "He would probably have been happier working in science. He's a trained marine biologist."

While Aunty Maiko and Uncle Hiroshi expressed sympathy for our emperor, I found it difficult. It was true he was forced to keep himself removed from the world; however, he was living in luxury and comfort. I suspected he wasn't forced to contend with the hardships and shortages that challenged the rest of Japan.

Of all the stories we told during our time in the cave, my favorite was Mama's. She told it again one day as we were drinking tea.

"Tell us how you met Papa," Harumi urged. "Please. I never grow tired of hearing it."

"You know I grew up here on Okinawa," Mama spoke between taking sips. "My father owned a market in Motobu—"

"Close to the ferry landing." Harumi interrupted.

"Yes, where the ferry from Iejima docked." Mama continued, "I worked for my father in the store and became acquainted with many of the customers." She set her cup down. "Hiroshi had already left Okinawa and traveled to Kyoto to seek his fortune as a silk merchant."

"What happened at your store?" Harumi was impatient for Mama to reach the exciting part.

"A young farmer from Iejima would come to shop. After several visits, he introduced himself to me. His name was Katsumi Oshiro. He came to the market more and more frequently, always to talk with me. My father would grumble and complain that Oshiro-san was keeping me from completing my work, but I knew he wasn't entirely serious in his objections. And I wasn't positive how I felt about the young man until one day." Mama picked up her empty cup. "Is there any more tea?"

"Yes, yes." I poured her another cup. "Go on, keep talking." I knew Mama liked to stretch a good story, probably just to hear us nudge her.

"I was organizing the melons a farmer had brought in that morning when I heard a commotion out on the street. Men were yelling, and a horse was stomping and whinnying. Imagine my surprise when I saw that one of the men was Katsumi. He had always been so quiet and polite before."

"*Yare*, what was going on?" Aunty Maiko asked.

"The other man was driving a wagon filled with scrap metal. His horse struggled with the heavy load, and had stopped. The man began beating the horse to make it continue. Katsumi stood in front of the animal and held its harness, shouting, 'That is no way to treat this fine horse' and 'You don't deserve to own such an animal.' Then he made the driver remove part of the load so the horse could pull the wagon. Katsumi stood in the street, watching the driver until he unloaded some of his cargo, drove the wagon away, and came back for the second trip. I was surprised that Katsumi was so forceful. When I saw him demonstrate how bravely he defended the poor horse and how he stood up to abuse, I understood his character and realized the depth of my feelings."

"What a wonderful story," Aunty Maiko said.

"Yes, and for the entire time we were married, I never had reason to alter my opinion."

As much as I loved the story, and remembered the strong, quiet man who had been my father, I always heard it with a little sadness. "And now he is gone," I said softly.

"Yes." Mama must have heard me. "But much of him lives on. Every time I look at you, Atsuko, I see the strong and generous person your father was. Harumi, your love of animals and your energy are qualities your father possessed. Remember that."

Mama's words made me think. Her ability to draw strength from her experiences, especially the losses, was always an inspiration—something I strived to emulate.

The injured stranger became more and more restless in the next few days. He started talking in actual words. One day while he was more agitated than usual, Aunty Maiko and I attempted to comfort him. Suddenly, the pilot's eyes fluttered, and he opened them wide, squinting at first against the light from the lantern.

"He's awake." Aunty Maiko addressed her words to Harumi, who was nearby.

The man stared at me without recognition. "Where am I? Why am I not dead?"

It may have partly been because of the light inside the cave, but when the young man gazed into my eyes and asked me his questions, all I heard was his flat tone and all I saw was an emptiness in his eyes. They chilled me to the bone.

Chapter 24

Tigers kill—no guilt.
Soldiers fight and lose their souls
to the gods of war.
—Atsuko Oshiro

Before the wounded pilot became completely alert, he periodically moaned and cried out. When he did, Uncle Hiroshi or Gorou propped him up while Mama carefully gave him water—a small amount at a time so he wouldn't choke. After the pilot regained consciousness, Mama kept us busy finding food and herbs she could prepare for him.

Following her directions, Harumi and I went down to the beach at low tide to gather *mozuku.* Since it was the middle of April, the seaweed grew abundantly in the shallows. Before we left the ledge, Uncle Hiroshi warned us to be careful and watch out for any planes or soldiers. However, it was peaceful down at the tide pools; far off in the distance, we saw an occasional plane, but none flew overhead. We rolled up our trousers and waded out where we could pull the feathery plants from the water. In a short time, we filled our basket with the brown algae Mama would make into soup. We didn't linger, but since it appeared safe, we did take the time to pick some mussels for our dinner that evening.

While Harumi and I were on the beach, Aunty Maiko and Uncle Hiroshi went up the path to the top of the cliff. Mama asked them to find *sannin.* She would use the leaves of the shell ginger to make a healing tea.

In the first few days of being awake, Mama gave the pilot only tea and broth. "He is so malnourished, he won't be able to tolerate solid food for a while."

The effort to drink the liquids exhausted him. After a few swallows, he would fall back asleep. On the fourth day, the pilot began to talk. Initially he was confused, didn't know where he was, or how he arrived. I wasn't surprised; he had gone from flying in bright sunlight to waking up in a darkened cave among strangers. Having suffered a blow to the head, along with his other injuries, further explained his dazed condition. Gradually his memory returned and his dazed expression faded.

"I am Oshiro-san." Mama introduced herself in a low, calm voice. "These are my daughters, Atsuko and Harumi." Mama pointed, first to me, then Harumi.

Harumi and I knelt beside Mama next to the man's futon where he lay, half-sitting up and propped by pillows. We gave him a short bow from the waist and smiled.

"I am Tadashi," he said. "Tadashi Sato."

"Do you remember anything that happened to you?" Mama asked.

"I was flying my plane." Tadashi spoke with great effort. "I had been ordered to Iejima."

"Oh." Harumi gasped. "Our home—" She saw Mama's frown and said no more.

"I was over the East China Sea when my engine started to sputter." Tadashi paused for breath, as though talking was painful. "I opened the throttle, but nothing happened. I turned the plane around and headed back to Okinawa." He stopped for another long pause. "Without any power, I couldn't control the plane, and it began to tip from side to side. The last thing I remember, I nosedived into trees. And here I am. Is this Okinawa?"

"Yes, this is Okinawa," Mama said. "You are safe now, with our family."

"I can't move my arm." Tadashi made a futile effort to lift his left arm, but it was bound to his chest by a strip of cloth.

"Don't struggle." Mama placed her hand on his arm. "Your arm is broken and in a splint. It needs to be kept in place in order to heal."

For the next few days, Tadashi slept most of the time. Mama said his body needed all his energy to recover from his injuries. When he was able to eat, she told us what would be good for him. From the trees up on the cliff, we picked *goya*. Mama cooked the bitter melon and fed it, along with rice wrapped in seaweed, to Tadashi. Gradually, he stayed awake for longer periods of time, and his strength improved.

When Tadashi first began to stand, Uncle Hiroshi or Gorou helped him. He was weak and complained of dizziness. Gradually he began to walk, but the only place he went was to our outdoor toilet concealed behind a clump of bushes on the far end of the ledge. At first, he needed help to use it. Even after he was able to walk there by himself, the effort exhausted him.

As Tadashi grew stronger, he talked more. Ever since he told us he was ordered to fly to Iejima, we were curious about what was happening on our island. One day as we finished our afternoon meal, he told us what he knew.

"After the Americans took control of Okinawa's northern peninsula, they invaded Iejima." Tadashi drew an outline of the island in the dirt and pointed to the beaches where the enemy had landed. "This is where they set up their camps." He marked a spot not far from the town. "And this is where Japanese are holed up." Tadashi indicated a ridge lined with caves. "Other Japanese are in trenches dug along the beaches. Many soldiers from both sides are on Iejima, and the fighting is intense."

"That means the damage must be extensive." Uncle Hiroshi's mouth was drawn tight in a grim expression. "What were your orders?"

"I was to fly into the American encampment and level as much of it as I could. Tents and people."

"All that fighting on our small island." Mama shook her head. "So much destruction. The Oshiro family has farmed there for generations. Now it could be gone."

I looked at Harumi. Tears ran down her cheeks. Without saying anything, she picked up Miss Singer and walked into the darkened room where we slept. I understood how she felt; when Tadashi said how many soldiers were on Iejima and the extent of the fight, a feeling of terrible loss and helplessness swept over me. *What will happen to our family? Even if we survive the war, we won't have a home.*

Not only did Tadashi talk more, as his strength increased, so did his appetite. One day he commented on the rice balls Mama made for lunch. "This meal is much better than what we were eating in the army. Not even the pilots ate this well. How were you able to buy good rice?"

"Gorou gave us this rice." Harumi spoke before anyone could stop her.

"It's a story with complications." Uncle Hiroshi hesitated. "I'm not sure—"

"It doesn't matter anymore," Gorou said. "Everyone can know." He turned to Tadashi and continued, "This rice was meant for the officers. The tobacco harvest was larger than expected, and Hiroshi gave me the surplus. He asked me to try to trade it for food."

"But not on the black market?" I asked, remembering how he had assured me he hadn't done that.

"No, not the black market," Gorou said. "I traded the extra tobacco for cigarettes from the Japanese Tobacco Company and sold them to army officers. I used the money to buy the rice from my friend who was a supply sergeant. He had gotten the rice from the officers' stores. By the time we finished our business, I had the rice, my friend had the money, and the officers had cigarettes."

"Not exactly legal." Uncle Hiroshi shook his head. "I thought it might be something like that."

"I couldn't tell anyone about it before, but now it doesn't matter—my friend is dead."

"I can understand why we find ourselves behaving less than honorably," Tadashi said. "The officers often make life miserable for the soldiers, and there is much resentment."

Not long after the conversation about how we acquired the rice, Tadashi began to change.

He became preoccupied by his honor, or what he perceived as his lack of honor. "I shouldn't have turned back when my plane failed. I should have kept going until my plane crashed, even if it was in the East China Sea."

"It doesn't do you any good to focus on that," Aunty Maiko said. "You're here now, and for the present, you are safe."

"But I failed to serve the emperor." Tadashi sat with his head bowed and resting in his hands.

As much as we tried to rid him of guilt, he wasn't comforted by our words. He became quieter and more withdrawn. Nightmares plagued him, and he cried out in agony while sleeping. Tadashi was jumpy and looked haggard.

As much as we tried to soothe his anxiety and attempted to speak calmly, and hopefully, about the future, it was difficult because we felt despondent about the war news. Knowing that Japan was losing control of Okinawa and our home might no longer exist discouraged us. All the time we spent in darkness, interrupted by fearful scrambling for food and water, began to take a toll on our spirits. What had been time spent telling stories of better days shifted into long periods of silence. Sometimes I had to ask Mama the same question more than once because her mind had drifted off. The added pressure of knowing Americans were not far away added to our sensations of dread. Our fears intensified within the gloom of the cave. For me, the cave changed; no longer a sanctuary from danger, it became a deadly trap.

With time on my hands, I occupied myself by writing in my Book of Days. Ever since my birthday in September, when I made a promise to myself, I had been more faithful in recording my thoughts and feelings. When I looked back at earlier entries, I saw how much our lives changed, and how my poetry reflected mostly grave thoughts. But not everything in my life was gloom and despair. I considered the joy I felt when Gorou revealed his feelings for me, and the intensity with which I returned those emotions. I attempted to describe what I felt. It was like the ache I experienced when I stood on the edge of the cliff at sunset and looked west. The sun, as it sank into the horizon, turned blue water into a sea of molten gold. As the day faded with a beautiful display of nature, it was as though it left behind a promise for tomorrow. Sadness at departure, anticipation for a return. I could only hope that someday, my future with Gorou would become reality. Unfortunately, other somber events forestalled our happiness.

One day at the beginning of June was unusually quiet. I didn't see planes, even in the far distance. We decided to eat out on the ledge and take advantage of the warm weather and clear skies. I don't remember what we talked about; it must have been nothing important. As we finished our meal, Tadashi stood up and walked past the shrubs concealing the toilet. He was gone a long time. Then I heard rustling, but couldn't see movement. The sound was followed by a shout, then nothing.

"Tadashi might have fallen." Harumi looked at me with a question in her eyes.

"Let's go and see." I stood and motioned for her to come with me.

We walked to the toilet, but there was no Tadashi. Bushes on the other side of the toilet had broken branches. We walked over to them.

"Be careful," I said. "We're close to the edge." Looking over the bushes, I saw where Tadashi had fallen. His broken body was splayed out on the rocks below. I gasped, and before I could shield her view, Harumi saw the dead pilot too. I grabbed her close and felt her shiver, even though the day was warm.

"Why did he do it?" she asked, over and over, between sobs. "I don't understand."

I thought back to the lifeless expression in his eyes when he first gained consciousness, and how quiet he became afterward. "We saved his body, but his soul was already dead."

After we told the others what we discovered, Uncle Hiroshi said he and Gorou should retrieve Tadashi's body. "It's not safe to leave it exposed," Uncle Hiroshi said. "It could lead soldiers to us."

"We must treat his body with respect," Aunty Maiko said. "Everyone deserves dignity."

"What should we do?" I asked.

"We could bury him at sea," Gorou said. "If I take my boat out, we can go out past the coral reefs, and he would sink into the depths."

It was decided that a burial at sea would be best. It preserved Tadashi's dignity and, hopefully, wouldn't jeopardize our safety. Aunty Maiko gave Uncle Hiroshi a silk sheet to wrap Tadashi's body and said they should gently slide him into the water.

Gorou and Uncle Hiroshi went down to the inlet and retrieved the boat. Mama, Aunty Maiko, Harumi, and I kept a vigil on the ledge—in the spot where Harumi and I stood earlier. From there we saw the two men carefully wrap Tadashi in the sheet and lift him into the boat. Together, Uncle Hiroshi and Gorou rowed out past the shelf of coral to deeper, darker water. Mama grabbed my and Harumi's hands. With Aunty Maiko holding Harumi's other hand, we made a line of mourners. We stood, gazing out to sea, and prayed for Tadashi Sato.

I said a funeral prayer I learned from the nuns at the Maryknoll Academy, and Harumi joined me. "Eternal rest give unto him, and let perpetual light shine upon him. May he rest in peace."

Mama and Aunty Maiko contributed a Buddhist saying:

What the caterpillar perceives is the end,
to the butterfly is just the beginning.
Everything that has a beginning has an ending.
Make your peace with that and all will be well.

As the days after Tadashi's burial passed, we continued our peculiar existence, confined in a small world and separated from everything else. By July, it had been more than two months since Tadashi dropped into our lives and Mr. Hano told us about the battle for Okinawa and how Americans controlled the northern peninsula. After that, we knew nothing more.

Then another problem added to our difficulties. We had very little rice left and became dependent on what we could find to eat. While there was food both on the beach and on top of the cliff, we were afraid to be out in the open. Not knowing what soldiers might be near us, we needed to be cautious anytime we left the cave. Our rare trips to the top of the cliff to forage for food and collect water took place after dusk. We didn't cross the meadow to the old farmhouse pump. Instead, we walked under the canopy of trees to stay hidden from any planes. We moved quickly along the exposed section of path leading from the ledge to the top. While sitting on the ledge, we stayed near the opening of the cave where overhanging rock sheltered us from sight. Our trips to the beach were hurried and occurred only on days we saw no planes.

The strain of living in fear and the necessity to ration our food began to take a toll. Instead of being distracted, Mama became short-tempered and snapped at us for what seemed to be trivial reasons. Harumi and I often quarreled with each other, and both of us grew impatient when Uncle Hiroshi interfered in our conversations. Even Aunty Maiko, the calmest of us, developed headaches and spent much of her time lying on her futon, a wet cloth stretched over her forehead. And it wasn't only our manners that deteriorated; our appearances changed.

Mama always expected Harumi and me to dress neatly and be as well-groomed as possible. We wore our hair in neat bobs, kept clean and shiny. Mama cut our hair until my aunt and uncle moved in with us. Then Aunty Maiko took over the task. Both Harumi and I preferred Aunty Maiko's efforts. Somehow, her haircuts resulted in a more stylish look than Mama's. But in the cave, hairstyles faded in importance, along with other aspects of our personal appearance.

For as long as I could remember, Mama wore her hair long, pulled back into a bun at the nape of her neck—every hair in place. But not anymore. Strands of hair escaped and hung loose. Not only that, but her hair that had been the same glossy black as mine, developed streaks of gray running through it. Outside, I noticed tiny lines around Mama's mouth and eyes had begun to carve themselves in her face.

When we first moved to the cave, it wasn't easy to adjust to living without a washroom and the opportunity to bathe. However, we had plenty of water and washed frequently. With our trips to the old farmhouse limited, water was too precious to waste, and we washed sparingly.

I found all these changes worrisome. Were we making the best of a terrible situation, or did it mean we had given up? What happens to a family that despairs? Can there be any good outcome for us? Or are we to be victims of a cruel fate?

Even though pressure and anxiety added to our difficulties, we struggled to maintain our safety and stay hidden. However, despite all precautions, our invisibility came to an end.

On a clear day near the end of July, we sat together in the main room of the cave. Outside, the air was typically humid, but we sat in relative coolness. Mama lit the lantern for a short while, and it gave enough light for us to work. Aunty Maiko took out her sewing kit and mended clothes; I sat with my portable desk and looked through my papers, while Uncle Hiroshi helped Harumi with her math. Gorou, stretched out on his futon, napped.

"Shh," Mama hissed suddenly. She held a finger in front of her mouth. "I hear something."

The four of us froze. I nudged Gorou from his sleep and held my hand over his mouth when he mumbled a protest.

The noise outside grew louder. People were on the ledge. I knew with a sinking heart that whoever it was, they would soon discover us. Once they saw our fire pit and water barrel, our presence would no longer be a secret. The voices became louder. They spoke English.

"What are they saying?" Mama asked me.

I tried to remember what I learned from Sister Mary Josephine, but it had been so long, I didn't comprehend everything I heard, but I relayed the part I understood. "They want whoever is in the cave to come out."

"Do they say what they plan to do?" Mama asked.

The voices outside continued.

"No," I said. "They won't do anything until the interpreter arrives. They think we have weapons. But they won't do anything until they can talk with us. I think I heard something about gas."

"We have no weapons," Uncle Hiroshi said. "They have us at their advantage. We'll have to leave—or be gassed."

"Wait." Aunty Maiko spoke for the first time. "We may have no choice, and our fate is waiting out on the ledge, but we have a choice for how we face it."

"What do you have in mind, Maiko?" Mama asked. "Tell us."

"If we are to be executed by the Americans, I think we should meet our death with pride. We dress in our finest, and when we reach the outside, we hold our heads high. No matter how frightened we are, we appear calm and brave. The Americans have the power to determine whether we live or die, but they do not have control over our spirits."

Quickly we changed into our best clothes. Uncle Hiroshi put on a black dress suit; Gorou had no suit, but had a clean shirt and pair of trousers. Harumi and I wore the jackets Aunt Maiko made and embroidered for our birthdays. Mama looked elegant in her kimono, black silk with silver stitching, traditional for women in Okinawa. Aunty Maiko, dignified as always, wore her green kimono.

Before we left the cave, Gorou came up to me and held my hand to his chest. "Whatever happens, remember I have always cared for you, and always will."

"I feel the same—always." I could feel his heart beating underneath my hand. A short moment that held all our tomorrows.

"Remember, pride and dignity," Aunty Maiko whispered loudly enough for all of us to hear.

In single file, we bent over and walked through the cave's opening. At first, I blinked in the bright sunlight and saw only the silhouetted outline of the soldiers. As my eyes adjusted to the light, I realized the soldiers didn't have their weapons pointed at us. Instead, the soldiers smiled. Lined up, with our heads held high, we received no threats and no violence. One of the soldiers did approach us, but only to pass out gum and chocolate.

I held the soldier's gift in my hand, unable to comprehend what I saw. I had been so frightened at the prospect of torture and death; I couldn't immediately grasp what was happening. The rest of my family must have had the same reaction. Nobody said anything, but stood there, with dazed looks.

With gestures and my limited English, we attempted to communicate with the American soldiers. Luckily, a soldier who spoke Japanese joined us. He explained the plan for us—being transported to a refugee camp. We had no choice, and could only hope wherever they took us was better than where we had been living. No matter what the future held for us, our ordeal of living in a cave was over.

OCTOBER, 1947

Chapter 25

We sift war's rubble
finding fragments of the past
to rebuild our lives.
—Atsuko Oshiro

Gorou gave me chrysanthemums on my twenty-first birthday. His gift reminded me of when he came to our farm with similar flowers the day I turned eighteen; it was the day I began to realize how much he meant to me. Many events in the three years between those two birthdays changed our lives, and I wasn't the same young girl anymore.

The day I turned twenty-one, we were in Naha. Gorou bought the flowers at a market stall in the Okinawan city. It was almost two years since we left the refugee camp and moved back to our farm on Iejima. Our return to the larger island was not like the previous time we came—to hide from the war as it wreaked havoc on our world. Instead of fearful retreat, we came with optimism.

When we were in the refugee camp, a doctor examined Gorou's damaged foot. He told us about the possibility of improving its condition. A specially made shoe would help straighten his foot and provide support. Second, an operation on the tendons and ligaments could put his foot in proper alignment. Gorou was fitted for the shoes, and in the two years he'd been wearing them, he had been able to move much more easily and almost pain free. With the success of the shoes, we held hopes the operation would complete the process of fixing his foot.

The prospect of mending Gorou's foot wasn't the only positive outcome of life in a refugee camp. Americans ran it, and with victory over Japan, they were able to provide for us much better than our own military could. By the time of our surrender, Japan was broken. We had struggled for so long with severe shortages, I don't know what our fate would have been if we hadn't received help. The situation contained a great deal of irony. Two countries, dedicated to destroying each other and working diligently to accomplish that, ultimately combined forces to rebuild the land they demolished and help the people who were victims.

When we left the cave, we were taken south in a truck carrying the six of us and all our possessions. Once settled in the cramped quarters of the camp, an American officer interviewed us in order to decide our future. Luckily, Mama had the documents proving ownership of our farm on Iejima. With the help of an interpreter, we established ourselves as legitimate landowners and, as such, were put near the top of a priority list.

The first trip back to Iejima was disheartening. Much of the island had been destroyed during the battle for Okinawa. Our house had been bombed and not much remained of the outbuildings. Initially we thought the refugee camp would be our home for an extended period of time. But because of our placement on the list, construction of our new house occurred fairly soon. We moved there in time to celebrate the New Year 1946.

Built by Americans, our new home was considerably different from the original. The biggest change was the addition of electricity. Having that convenience provided an enormous improvement in the way we lived. No more woodstove or oil lamps. A water heater provided hot water instantly. After nearly a year in the cave and the camp, the opportunity to bathe was a joy. Soaking in the tub and feeling clean was a luxury I never again took for granted. One of the first things Uncle Hiroshi purchased was a new radio, and we could hear broadcasts from Kyoto and Tokyo. From months of living without knowing anything beyond our existence in the cave, the radio reconnected us to the outside world.

However, with all its new features, there were aspects I missed from the original house. Mama's shrine wasn't the same. She fashioned a nook and hung the scroll above the stones memorializing our ancestors, but it was a long time before it felt as sacred as the alcove in our other home. None of our furniture survived the war. The *tansu* where I kept my clothes was gone. It had been in our family for many generations, and I missed the beautiful chest carved from wood and darkened with age. At least I saved my portable desk and its treasures: the book of poetry given to me by the nuns; my Book of Days with its entries for 1945; and the jewelry Harumi and I had been given by Mama—all had been kept safe.

The worst loss of all was Mr. Nishiyama. He did not survive, nor did his house. I knew he was given the opportunity to come with us and chose not to, but that didn't stop me from feeling sorry about his death. Every time I walked by his farm, I felt twinges of grief for our kind neighbor, now gone.

Gradually, men returned from the war. Their arrival made it possible for Mama to hire extra help for the farm. Two benefits emerged from having more workers. Mama contacted Mr. Nishiyama's nephew and began to negotiate the purchase of the farm next to ours. Gorou, released from farming, was able to resume fishing—the occupation that made him happiest.

In March, three months after we moved back home, Gorou and I married. Our hopes, tested by war, flourished in the new peace. The joy we found in each other fulfilled all the promises we made during the desperate times now behind us.

Initially, we lived in the cottage Mamoru and his wife had occupied. Luckily, the small building had escaped damage. For the first time in my life, I was the mistress of my own home. During my early days as Gorou's wife, he exhibited great patience as I learned the skills of keeping house. He never once complained about the poor meals I placed before him. Fortunately, I seldom made the same mistake twice, and eventually my cooking improved.

One day, while I fed the chickens and looked for eggs, I glanced up and saw a familiar figure walk up the driveway.

"Sayuri!" I dropped the basket of feed and ran to meet her. We hugged, and then I held her at arm's length. "You've changed. You're still Sayuri, but you look older, like all of us." My friend had become thinner, and she didn't look like the girl who always appeared to be on the brink of laughter. Her face had a new, serious, expression.

"We've all changed," Sayuri said. "It has been a cruel time."

"Come sit down." I led her to a bench. "What happened to you? I only ever received one letter—almost two years ago."

"Many things happened, most of them bad. I remember I wrote about shortages. They became worse. We suffered greatly. I feel terrible, but our situation was so desperate, I sold the pearl. If I hadn't, we would have starved. I'm so sorry."

"The necklace is gone?" My immediate reaction was disappointment. How could she? Then I realized the necklace served a purpose if it saved Sayuri's family. After all, I only bought it as a souvenir of a vacation, and here was Sayuri, alive and back on Iejima. "I'm glad the pearl was able to help you. I still have the pendant you gave me. I cannot tell you how many times I felt for it, resting above my heart. I would rub the elephant and ask for courage whenever we faced danger." I went on and told her about our family's adventures—leaving the farm, living in a cave, and then the refugee camp.

"Your farm looks different." Sayuri looked around. "Mostly new buildings—a new house. We have a new home too. My father regained his job. He's back in charge of the ferry service. You will have to come visit us."

"The house isn't the only new thing," I said. "I'm married now. Do you remember Gorou?"

"You married Gorou?" Sayuri smiled and gave me another hug. "I always thought the two of you belonged together. Do you like being married?"

"I'm happy, living with Gorou. I don't know if he feels the same way when he has to eat my meals. I hope someday you are as fortunate as I am. But tell me about yourself. I heard not many people in the camps survived."

"It's true." Sayuri spoke in a low tone, and lines of sadness formed on her face. "Did you hear about the grenades?"

"Yes." I nodded, thinking of the stories in the refugee camp about how the Japanese military issued grenades to civilians so they could commit suicide. Others were encouraged to hang themselves. I even learned mothers strangled their own children.

"For girls, the future was bleak. Do you know about the comfort women?" She went to tell me about girls she knew who were recruited as patriots to help the Japanese army and forced to become prostitutes for soldiers. "My fate was horrible enough, but at least I was spared from becoming a comfort woman."

"Did you stay with your family?"

"No, I was taken to be a Princess Lily. Many people lived in caves, trying to live through the battle for Okinawa. Some of them were evicted so the army could have the caves. Wounded soldiers were treated there. The Princess Lilies were the nurses taking care of the sick and the dying."

"Were you trained?" I thought back to what Mama had done for Tadashi with his broken arm, and I knew I could never have done that.

"No. Officers would shout at us what to do without explaining how to do it. The caves were dark. With all the wounded, the smell was horrible. Some of the rooms were low, and we had to crawl on our hands and knees through filth. Constant screams of pain echoed off the rock walls as we tried to aid the injured. The main medical care given to the soldiers was amputation. At night we had to take the severed body parts away and find a safe place to deposit them. It would be late, and I'd be so tired my bones ached, but I'd stand on the edge of a cliff to toss arms and legs into the sea. The next day, it would be the same routine. This went on for four months."

As Sayuri told me her story, I understood the sadness etched on her face. She faced a gruesome situation and been forced to perform despicable tasks. The girl who laughed easily and found humor in almost everything was gone. I only hoped that the horror she had lived with didn't take permanent residence in her heart.

"I'm so glad you survived." I struggled to find the right words to comfort my friend. After the atrocities she experienced, I didn't want to speak in trite platitudes. "What about your brothers?"

"They didn't return, and we never heard what happened to them." Sayuri almost whispered her answer. "For a long time we hoped for their return, or to at least hear what happened. But the end of the war was so chaotic, no one received any information."

"I'm so sorry." I reached out and held my friend's hand. "Your poor mother. How is she?"

"Not good. Mostly she sits and stares out the window. It's as though she thinks if she keeps waiting, Junichi and Nobu will come walking up the path. Papa's not much better. It's impossible to talk to either one of my parents about the war."

"What about you? Do you have any plans? Are you going to live here?"

"I'm not sure. For the present, I'm staying here and helping my family. But I can't live here forever. I need to take care of myself. I'd like to go back to Okinawa and become trained—maybe for an office job. Definitely not a nurse."

The afternoon slid into evening as we talked on the porch, and Gorou would be home in a short while. I invited Sayuri to stay for dinner, not promising anything special. She declined the invitation, saying she wanted to be home before dark; her parents expected her.

For the next few months, we saw each other frequently; however, in July, Sayuri left Iejima. She enrolled in a secretarial training course. With the presence of American troops on Okinawa, many Japanese women worked at the bases, and Sayuri had hopes to acquire such a job.

As always, Gorou worked long hours, and by the time I became pregnant, he saved enough money for materials to build our own house. Not too far from Mama's house, and on the way toward town, our new home stood on a small rise. A porch wrapped three sides. I could sit facing east in the morning and see the sunrise; in the evening, I watched the sun disappear in the west. I experienced anticipation for the coming day and thankfulness for the day just past.

Our baby was born in June 1947. Discomfort and illness accompanied my pregnancy, and the delivery brought great pain, but the agony of childbirth faded with the first cries of the newborn. The image of Gorou when he looked down at his child would never leave me. Through all the terrible events we experienced, and all the suffering Gorou endured, I had never seen him cry. Until he saw his daughter.

"What's the matter?" At first I thought something was terribly wrong.

"When I married you, I gained a family." Gorou picked up the baby and held it close. "And now I have someone who is part of me. She's perfect. No one could be happier."

Gorou and I were not the only ones excited for the arrival of Nozomi. Harumi spent as much time with her as she could. Maryknoll Academy had reopened, and Harumi was once again a student. I didn't think she resented school as much as she had on Okinawa, but she begrudged the time it required. Every day, as soon as school let out, Harumi rushed to my house to play with my daughter. Harumi claimed her presence was necessary because only she could teach the folktales from Papa and explain how to take care of animals. Harumi would walk all over the farm, with the baby on her back, talking constantly to her. Quite often, Miss Singer was part of the parade, joining in with a chorus of meows.

Four months after our child's birth, the three of us traveled to Okinawa. A bus took us from the ferry landing to Naha, where we would stay while Gorou had his operation. The day before he checked into the hospital, we took a trip to a memorial site located on a cliff in the southeastern corner of Okinawa.

Leaving the bus, we walked several miles over a well-worn path to Mabuni Hill, a place where many lives had ended in the final days of the war. The journey turned into a pilgrimage as I thought about what had happened there a little over two years before. We both walked quietly, speaking very little. Even the baby, carried in the blanket that kept her strapped to my back, was silent. We reached the edge of the cliff and stood gazing out at the Pacific Ocean. The longer we stood, the stronger I felt the significance of this place. I began to cry.

"So many lives lost." Looking down, I could see rocks washed over by the powerful waves of the Pacific. Thousands of Japanese who jumped from the cliffs had died on those rocks, and the waves carried their broken bodies out to sea. They plunged to their deaths at the urging of the Japanese government. Deaths citizens were told would preserve their honor and allow them to escape torture from the Americans. "We are looking east—where each morning the rising sun assures us of the future. What about the lost futures of so many?"

For years I never fully understood Mama and her ties to our ancestors. For her, their spirits were always with us. For me, while I never questioned their existence, I also never fully believed in them. Until that day. As I stood where so many people had died, I felt the presence of their spirits as I had never done before. "It's all so tragic."

Gorou stepped behind me and carefully took our daughter from the blanket holding her.

"We can't change the past or bring back the dead." He held the baby so I could look at her sleeping. "Look instead at what we have. Think about her name."

"Nozomi."

"Hope. We gave her that name because we are looking to the future with hope for a better life, with hope for peace. She is our rising sun."

Gorou's words comforted me. While I would always feel sorrow for the destruction and losses of the war, I knew with the support of my family and the love of my husband, I could anticipate a better future.

Hope for tomorrow:
The land of the rising sun
will prosper again.
(Atsuko Oshiro)

Glossary

ama. pearl diver
asa. sea lettuce; type of seaweed
baka. stupid
bento. box for carrying food
bogor. pineapple found on Okinawa
bushido. ancient Japanese code of honor for warriors
cha. tea
daikon. large white radish
daimyo. feudal rulers below the status of shogun
futon. cotton mattress used as a bed
Ginoza. city on the island of Okinawa
goya. bitter melon
hime. princess
hirami. thin-skinned, flat lemon
Hokkaido. prefecture in northern Japan
Honshu. largest island in Japan
Iejima. small island off the northwest coast of Okinawa
iwa. rock
Iwo Jima. one of the three volcano islands
kabocha. winter squash
kakebuton. quilt used on a futon
kamaboka. fish cakes
kamikaze. pilot on a suicide mission
kappogi. apron
Keizai Keisatsu. Economic Police
Kouri Island. island off the northern coast of Okinawa
kurigohan. steamed rice with chestnuts

kyanpu o suro. camping
Kyoto. major city located in central Honshu
Mitsumame. dessert with fruit
Miyako. island off the southeastern coast of Okinawa
mochi. dessert made with sweet bean paste
mozuku. seaweed
nekoyangai. cattails
Okinawa. prefecture in southern Japan
omikugi. paper fortunes
origiri. rice balls
rentan. charcoal briquettes
Rikugun Jun-I. warrant officer in the Japanese Imperial Army
Ryukyu Islands. islands in southern Japan; Okinawa is the main island
sake. alcoholic beverage made from fermented rice
sannin. edible plant; shell ginger
seijitsu. sincere, honest
sento. public baths
shisa. dog-lions; house guardians
shogun. military commander-in-chief in feudal Japan
shogunate. government under the rule of shoguns
shoujiki. integrity
shulan jiketsu. honorable suicide
soba. noodles made from buckwheat flour
sufu. fabric made from cotton fibers and wood pulp
tansu. Japanese wooden chest of drawers
tatami. floor mat
tengu. legendary creature; dog
tomagoyaki. omelette
tomodachi. friend
Touji. winter soltice celebration
Tsukemonoki. glass jar used for fermenting/pickling vegetables
ubagai. clam
umi budo. seaweed known as sea grapes
wagashi. dessert
wakame. edible seaweed

yare *or* **yare, yare**. idiom meaning "goodness" *or* "oh my goodness"
yoi. expression meaning "good"
yuzu. yellow/green citrus fruit

About the Author

Frances Snyder has always lived in the Pacific Northwest. Her summers as a child were spent on a small island in Puget Sound. Swimming, boating, and beachcombing took up most of her time there. The rest of the time she could be found curled up with a book. Frances has taught junior high school and worked in the Tacoma Public Library. Currently, she lives in Lacey, Washington, where she volunteers in a library, runs a program that presents book reviews, and spends time writing. The inspiration for *Chrysanthemum Girl* came from a coworker's stories about her mother during World War II in Okinawa.

CPSIA information can be obtained
at www.ICGtesting.com
Printed in the USA
FSHW011024180419
57379FS